EATING
FROM THE
GROUND
UP

Also by Alana Chernila

THE HOMEMADE
PANTRY

THE HOMEMADE
KITCHEN

EATING
FROM THE
GROUND
UP

recipes for simple,
perfect vegetables

———

ALANA
CHERNILA

photographs by Johnny Autry

CLARKSON POTTER/PUBLISHERS
New York

FOR MAIA,
WHO LOVES THE BITTER AND THE SWEET

———————

Jessie cut the top off the vegetables
and washed them in the brook.

"I'll put them in after the meat has
cooked a while," she said.

Soon the water began to boil, and the stew
began to smell good. . . . Now and then
Jessie stirred the stew with a big spoon.

"It will make a good meal," said Henry.

—GERTRUDE CHANDLER WARNER, *THE BOXCAR CHILDREN*

CONTENTS

WARMTH AND COMFORT

CELEBRATIONS AND OTHER EXCUSES TO EAT WITH YOUR HANDS

INTRODUCTION

"BUT WHAT'S THE BEST WAY TO EAT A RADISH?"

On my first day at the farmers' market, this question kept coming. It was spring, and the farm I worked for only had a few vegetables that early in the season. One side of the table held a tower of radish bunches, and the other, a basket of bagged baby arugula. When my first customer held a bunch of radishes and asked me for direction, I did my best to answer.

"Throw them into a salad? Slice them up and dip them in hummus?"

I didn't make the sale, and the truth was, I didn't really know what he was asking. Of course I liked vegetables, but I thought of them mostly as something that needed to be used up before spoiling in the fridge, packed into dishes to up their nutritious value, or snuck into a dish so I could feel better about how I was feeding my children. I knew that there were hundreds of ways to eat a radish, but I couldn't imagine that there were a few great ways to truly highlight all the wonderful flavors and the crunch that only a radish can provide. I didn't know how much radishes change as the sun gradually infuses them with spice over the course of the spring, that the delicate snap of a fresh spring radish only holds a shadow of the heat that will come in late June, and that its mild and refreshing earthiness needs only a little lemon and some herbs to make it shine. But I took a few bunches home that week, and the next Saturday, when someone asked me my favorite way to eat a radish, I was ready.

"Make radish butter! Chop them up fine and fold them into soft butter with some crunchy salt, parsley, and a little lemon juice."

I think the whole town ate radish butter that week.

Each week that first summer, I'd take vegetables home from one market to prepare for the next, studying up in anticipation of the following week's questions. That first year turned into nearly a decade of working at the market, and answering those questions have become my favorite part of what I do. Because, although there are countless ways to eat our vegetables, there are a few perfect ways to make each vegetable sing. These are the recipes I share the most, and you'll find every one of them here in this book.

What would I do if I could only make cauliflower one way for the rest of my life? That's an easy one: roast in a hot oven with olive oil and cumin seeds. Cucumbers? There's nothing like rice vinegar and a little chopped dill to bring out the sweetness and crunch. Try mint and crushed red pepper flakes if you're serving pork, or a Japanese *sunomono* version with wakame and sesame to serve alongside home-made maki rolls or chicken teriyaki. Or my favorite, the versatile and affordable cabbage: Treat it like an onion and caramelize it on the stovetop. Add a little stock, top with yesterday's baguette and some grated cheese, and Caramelized Cabbage Soup (page 100) will soon take onion soup's place as a favorite cold-weather staple.

Plant-based eating is having a moment right now, and as a nation of eaters we're integrating greater numbers of vegetables into our diet, for reasons of both health and sustainability. We hide sweet potatoes in baked goods, blend kale into smoothies, and buy special gadgets to pass off zucchini as noodles. But the more I've searched for new ways to help people eat their vegetables, the less I've needed to hide them or dress them up in my cooking. As I discover the recipes that truly bring out the best in each root and leaf, I find myself craving the dishes that spotlight plants again and again. We don't need to disguise our vegetables; we just need to prepare them well.

This book is a collection of those perfect recipes I've discovered and shared over the years. These are the recipes that bring out the flavor and texture of a vegetable, using it to its fullest potential. My goal isn't health or sustainability, although eating more vegetables happens to contribute to both. Most of all, I love vegetables because they are so good, and these recipes focus on the pleasure they bring to my table.

WHERE TO PICK YOUR VEGETABLES

It's a great time to love vegetables, because beautiful vegetables are *everywhere*. When I was a kid, my grandparents had a backyard garden that supplied them with the produce they needed for the breakfasts at their bed-and-breakfast. At that time, gardening was the best way to get fresh food that was out of the normal supermarket rotation. These days, gardening is still a good way to do it, but it's just one of so many great options, from farmers' markets to farm stands, and from Asian groceries to regular supermarkets. Let's talk through some of these resources and what to look for when you're there.

FARMERS' MARKETS: At this point, there are more than 5,000 farmers' markets in the United States, and the number continues to rise. This means that there's a farmers' market in or near most communities, and in larger towns and cities, there are often several markets that convene on various days. These markets are defined by direct sales between farmers and customers, but beyond that, they are as diverse as the communities that shop at them. Some, like the Union Square Greenmarket in New York City, are sprawling, comprehensive, and incredibly competitive for vendors. Others might be four or five stalls that set up for a few hours each Saturday. However your market fits into this spectrum, there are some real perks to buying your vegetables at the farmers' market:

1. The vegetables are fresh, typically harvested in the last 24 to 36 hours. This not only means that veggies will taste better, but it also means that they'll last longer once they get to your kitchen.

2. You can find varieties of vegetables you wouldn't find at the supermarket. Most supermarket vegetables are grown for transport, and that system favors vegetables that can stand up to a week on a train or several days in the back of a truck.

3. Your money is going straight to the farmer. Farmers' markets give farmers a venue to sell directly to consumers. You might buy their product for three bucks at the supermarket or three bucks at the farmers' market, but the profit margin changes dramatically for them if there is no middleman. This helps to make farming on a small scale a viable financial option, which is good for local economies, food systems, and the farmers themselves.

4. Farmers' markets are also great places to shop if you receive SNAP, WIC, or SFMNP benefits (that's Supplemental Nutrition Assistance Program; Women, Infants, and Children; and Senior Farmers' Market Nutrition Program, respectively). Many markets actually double your dollars, and it's a smart way to buy really good produce while getting federal dollars into the hands of small farmers.

CSA: CSA stands for *community supported agriculture,* and many small farms work on this model. Essentially you buy a share at the beginning of the season, and this investment enables the farmer to get the season started. Weekly shares usually begin when the growing season is in full swing. Some farms require pickup at the farm, and others deliver to your home or a central location.

While there's often a choice between certain vegetables, you tend to get what you get. This can be a real plus, as it often forces you to get out of cooking ruts and learn about new veggies you might not choose at the store. There might also be a pick-your-own component, and there can be added packages, from flowers to meat. This can be a very affordable option if you break the cost down to a weekly figure, as long as having new and exciting vegetables is a plus.

FARM STANDS: There's nothing more poetic than a roadside farm stand. Many small farms operate stands as a way to bring in extra income and make their produce available to the local community. You can often find gorgeous peak produce at a farm stand. Note that some farms will bus in produce from other places, and a charming wooden shack doesn't say anything about growing practices. If your priorities direct you to local, unsprayed, or organic produce, it's still a good idea to ask the farmer or person tending the stand.

SUPERMARKETS: Most of us primarily buy our veggies in the supermarket, and it's good to know what to look for.

Head toward the food that looks as close to the way it might have looked when it was picked. Check the stems of everything from broccoli to kale to herbs—the tighter and better looking the stem, the fresher the vegetable. Avoid food that's been drenched over and over with mist, as it tends to get waterlogged. Stick to vegetables that are unwrapped when possible, and keep in mind that the more whole you buy the veggies, the longer they'll last. These days there is chopped *everything* available, and while that can be a great time-saver, many of those vegetables have been exposed to the air and have started to degrade. Instead, do your precutting and washing when you get home. This small time investment right after shopping creates your own convenience foods that are fresher and less expensive.

INTERNATIONAL MARKETS: It's always a good idea to explore the produce section of international markets. You'll often find greens and roots you rarely find elsewhere, and they're great resources for hard-to-find herbs like shiso and curry leaf. You can also learn so much about new vegetables in these stores. If you see something unfamiliar, ask about how to prepare and cook it.

Fairytale Eggplant
$4/pint

ON LABELS

The land of food labeling can be tricky to navigate. Is it organic? Is it local? Is it non-GMO? Each of these standards is complex, and I urge you to use them as tools to prioritize how to choose your food, not as divisions between "right" food and "wrong." The more we know about how these labels reflect our own priorities, the more informed our choices will be. Do your best to buy the food that feels right for you and your family, and be wary of messages that make you feel guilty or, even more, inspire you to judge others.

That being said, the "organic" label comes with a list of requirements that can provide peace of mind. Organic food has been grown without traditional chemicals, and a certain amount of thought has gone into the creation of that vegetable. This is often worth the extra bit of money at the grocery store, if you are able to make that work. And the more we support organic farming practices by buying the fruits and vegetables of that labor, the more that movement will grow.

If you're buying directly from a farmer, ask them about their growing practices. Some might be certified organic, but others might grow according to organic practices without having the official stamp of approval. Keep an eye out for the Certified Naturally Grown label, a standard based on the National Organic Program but structured to make it easier and more affordable for small farms to apply. Some farms might do a mix of conventional and organic practices, and they're usually really happy to share their reasons and methods.

HOW TO WASH, STORE, AND MAKE YOUR VEGGIES LAST

Few things are as sad in the kitchen as a fridge full of rotted vegetables. Luckily, there are ways to wash and store your produce that can extend its freshness and make it easier to use when you're ready.

ASPARAGUS: If you plan to use the spears within 24 hours, put them in a glass with about an inch of water, and leave it on the counter. Otherwise, store in plastic in the refrigerator for 3 to 4 days. Wash asparagus tips well, as grit can stick in the feathered layers.

BROCCOLI AND CAULIFLOWER: Store whole in plastic bags or reusable containers in the refrigerator. Run the whole head under water before using.

BRUSSELS SPROUTS: Even if you buy your Brussels sprouts pastorally on their stalk, remove the sprouts from the stalk and store them in a plastic bag or reusable container in the refrigerator. No need to wash them—just remove the outer leaves.

CABBAGES: These can be stored naked in the refrigerator for several weeks. Remove any withered leaves before using. You can also use some of the cabbage and store the remaining section naked in the fridge. The section you cut will scar over, but you can just slice that bit off and discard it before using the rest. Don't wash cabbage—just remove the outer leaves.

CELERY: Store in plastic in the refrigerator. Save any leaves for stock, as they're flavor powerhouses.

CUCUMBERS: If the cucumbers were just picked or bought recently from a farmers' market, store them at room temperature for up to 2 days. After that, or if they weren't quite fresh when you bought them, store in plastic in the refrigerator.

GARLIC: Storing garlic long-term is a bit tricky, as it likes it about 40°F and humid (colder and wetter than potatoes or winter squash). If you grow your own garlic or buy it in bulk, the best way to find the ideal spot is to experiment with various corners of your house or basement. I've had it keep well in the little stairwell under my bulkhead door. Garlic can also be frozen with great success. Separate and peel the cloves, toss them in olive oil, put them in freezer-safe containers or bags and freeze. Pull out frozen cloves, let them thaw for a few minutes on the counter, and chop them up as you would fresh.

HEARTY GREENS (such as kale, Swiss chard, collards): Store these in a plastic bag or reusable container in the produce drawer of your refrigerator. Be sure to remove any slimy or rotten bits, as the decay will quickly spread to the other leaves. Greens can be washed and dried directly when you get home, or you can wash them just before cooking. Wash by soaking in the sink or a large bowl with a splash of vinegar. Greens can also be blanched and frozen for future use (see page 44).

HERBS: Place herbs in jars of water, like flowers, in the refrigerator. Put a plastic bag over the foliage. Basil doesn't like the cold, so it should be stored similarly, but leave it out on the counter.

LEEKS: Store leeks whole in plastic bags in the refrigerator. When you're ready to use them, chop off the stringy root and the toughest part of the green, and place those parts in a bag in the freezer to use for future stock. Chop the leek as the recipe prescribes. To wash, soak chopped leeks in water with a splash of distilled water, wine, or cider vinegar for 2 to 3 minutes, then scoop them out of the water with a slotted spoon.

LETTUCES AND TENDER GREENS: Buy lettuce heads whole, then separate out the leaves and wash and dry them right away. Feel free to mix varieties and create your own lettuce mixes. Store in a plastic or glass container with a dry paper towel in the refrigerator. I find that prewashing lettuce makes it more convenient for me to eat more lettuce more often.

ONIONS: Store cured onions in a cool, dark, well-ventilated place. Fresh eating onions should be stored in plastic in the refrigerator and used within 2 weeks.

POTATOES AND SWEET POTATOES: Store these roots out of the sun in a cool, dry place. The ideal temperature for them is between 45°F and 55°F, which is warmer than the fridge but cooler than most spots in your home. Potatoes also need good ventilation to prevent sprouting, so avoid storing them in plastic. A paper bag, box, or basket works well. Sweet potatoes and potatoes will sprout or rot if they don't have the right conditions, so it's best to buy just what you can use in a week or two if you don't have a good place to store them

Scrub potatoes and sweet potatoes just before you use them. Sometimes fresher potatoes from a farmer will be coated in dirt. Leave the dirt on until just before you use them—it helps to protect the potato.

ROOT VEGETABLES (such as beets, turnips, carrots, radishes): Separate the green tops from the roots and store separately in plastic bags or reusable containers in the refrigerator. You can wash and dry the tops right away, but wait to wash the roots until just before you cook them. Some root vegetables—like beets and carrots—will keep for up to 2 months in the refrigerator. Other more delicate roots, like white turnips and smaller radishes, should be used within a week or two.

SUMMER SQUASH: Store at room temperature and use within 3 days; otherwise store in the refrigerator. They degrade pretty quickly, so don't overbuy. Zucchini can be grated raw and frozen in a freezer bag for future zucchini bread (see page 252).

TOMATILLOS: Store fresh tomatillos at room temperature in their husks and use within 3 days; otherwise, store in the refrigerator.

TOMATOES: Store at room temperature; never refrigerate a tomato. If your tomatoes aren't quite ripe, store them stem-side down on the windowsill. Tomatoes can also be roasted and frozen for future use (see page 155).

WINTER SQUASH: Most squash that you buy at the supermarket or from a farmer will be cured or "hardened off," which means that they will keep for several months under the right conditions. Store squash, like potatoes, in a well-ventilated cool, dry place. Any squash with blemishes needs to be used quickly, as those spots will spread. If you use a section of a squash and want to save the rest for later, cover the flesh side with plastic wrap and store in the fridge for up to 5 days. Half squashes can also go into a freezer bag in the freezer.

VEGETABLES WITH CHEESE

This is not a vegetarian book, and it's even less of a vegan book. In fact, during the time we were eating these recipes every day, my younger daughter suggested we should call this book *Vegetables with Cheese.* She was not complaining, of course. She'd live on Cheesy Broccoli (see page 51) if she could, and I imagine she probably will when she sets out on her own and has to feed herself.

But why all this cheese and dairy?

Vegetables keep secrets, and to prepare them well we need to know how to coax those secrets out. It's such a pleasure to eat many freshly harvested vegetables plain, and anyone who's spent a blissful few minutes plucking warm-from-the-sun cherry tomatoes or sweet snap peas from their tangled vines will tell you this. In their best state, most vegetables don't need a thing to be delicious. But even then there are secret flavors in the background, a sweetness or pucker that Parmesan cheese or cream will bring into the light. As the vegetables get farther away from the ground, into the farmers' market or the supermarket, these secrets become more hidden, but they're still there. Trying to do our best with hairy carrots from the five-pound bag or a tired head of broccoli, it's important to have tools and tricks in our refrigerator and pantry. Ingredients like butter, crème fraîche, and cheese are excellent at helping vegetables sing.

In truth, it's not just dairy that does the job. There are several ingredients that enhance vegetables and let those secret flavors shine:

VEGETABLES WITH SALT: There is not one vegetable that doesn't perk up with a sprinkle of salt. Salt helps to bring the tomato-ness out of a tomato, and the cucumbery-ness out of a cucumber. In this book we'll be using two kinds of salt: basic kosher for cooking and larger flake sea salt for finishing. I specify these in the ingredients list so we can have a common saltiness measure, but if you prefer other kinds of salt, that's okay, too.

Salt enhances flavors, but it also helps to draw water out of vegetables. We'll use it to quick-pickled cucumbers (see page 31), tenderize cabbage (see page 59), or to dry out broccoli before roasting (page 50).

VEGETABLES WITH FAT: We'll use oil and butter to cook, but fat also functions as a flavor enhancer. Add butter to quickly braised collards or cabbage (see page 62) to provide richness without heaviness, calling out the nuttiness and sweetness in each leaf. Tomatoes drink in olive oil and use it to their best advantage, infusing it and transforming it into the ideal dressing. Oil and butter also soften the bite of bitter vegetables like arugula, radicchio, and broccoli raab, making way for the floral flavors that hide below the initial wave of bitter.

Oil and butter lend well to infusion, and this is a trick we'll use a lot in this book. Rosemary-infused oil really makes the Kale and White Bean Soup (page 108) special, and infusing butter with apple cider vinegar and garlic is my favorite dressing for collards (see page 49). I use unsalted butter, so I can control the salt in my recipes. When I call for olive oil, you can use whatever you have in your pantry. Fancy finishing is enhanced by fruitier, more expensive olive oils, but only if you're up for the splurge. I often call for neutral oil, and you can use whatever doesn't have much of a taste—grapeseed, sunflower, safflower, and canola are all good options. You'll also see many recipes in this book that call for Asian sesame oil. This is different from regular sesame oil, as it is more flavorful and slightly toasted. If you have toasted sesame oil, that will work, too.

VEGETABLES WITH ACID: Common cooking acids are lemon or lime juice, vinegar, ferments like tamari or soy sauce, and some dairy items like buttermilk or yogurt. Acids provide a counterpoint to sweetness, which helps to bring out that very same sweetness. Often when a dish is missing something, it's an acid that fills the void.

I use several vinegars in this book, but the most commonly used are rice vinegar (which adds acid without too much pucker), red wine vinegar (which is inexpensive and versatile), and balsamic. Balsamic is a treat, and it's easy to find a good one for not much money. Look for balsamic vinegar without any coloring or additives, and with "cooked grape juice" as its first ingredient.

AND, OF COURSE, VEGETABLES WITH DAIRY: Cream and vegetables are an age-old partnership, and we'll make good use of it. But also get ready for lots of Parmigiano-Reggiano, which brings salt, acid, and a bit of funkiness all at once. Look for hunks of the real stuff from Italy in your supermarket. They often go on sale and will last forever in the fridge. I'll refer to this as Parmesan cheese throughout the book, and if you can't buy the real stuff, feel free to substitute with less-expensive pecorino or Romano cheese. We'll also use lots of other cheeses in this book—from punchy Cheddar to creamy ricotta and mozzarella. I'm a big fan of yogurt and buttermilk, too, as the tang and creaminess make a great base for dressings.

THE TOOLS OF
THE KITCHEN

The recipes in this book are unfussy and versatile, and my hope is that you can execute them with nothing much more than a good knife, a pot, a functioning oven, and occasionally a blender. But good equipment can make faster work out many of these recipes, and I'd love to highlight some of the most used tools and gadgets that can help.

FOR CHOPPING AND BLENDING

KNIVES: A good knife is essential, and it will make all the difference when it comes to prepping vegetables. My favorite all-purpose knife is a 6-inch chef's knife, but find one that feels comfortable in your hand. A smaller paring knife is good to have, too. Be sure to keep your knives sharp. Many supermarkets offer free sharpening at the butcher counter, if you ask.

PEELERS: Vegetable peelers are inexpensive, and I like to have two so I can have company while peeling potatoes. Find a basic model and replace it when it gets rusty or dull. I also love soft-skin peelers, which have corrugated blades for peeling peaches, pears, and even tomatoes.

MANDOLINES: This is the tool that sends the most people to the ER, so I urge caution! I also encourage you not to be afraid of them, because for those of us with subpar knife skills, they are the best way to get consistently thin cuts of a vegetable. My favorite mandoline is made by Kyocera and costs about $20. I can slice a cucumber paper thin in about ten seconds. Don't ever try to cut all the way down to the end of the vegetable, as this is when fingertips are lost. Instead, stop when you're still comfortable, and chop the rest.

FOOD PROCESSORS: My Cuisinart is great for blending, but I use it more for its grating and chopping disks. Carrots and zucchini can be grated with no work at all, and you can grate a whole pound of cheese without breaking a sweat. Keep in mind that the grate will be a bit coarser than what you would get with a box grater. The standard slicing disk that comes with most food processors makes a nice thin and regular cut, and there are additional disks to buy if you want different sizes.

BLENDERS: Any of the blended recipes in this book can be made with a regular blender or a high-speed blender like a Vitamix. High-speed blenders tend to have a higher capacity, so they can often handle a recipe in one batch, whereas a regular blender usually requires two.

GRATERS: A box grater does most of the grating you need, as long as you don't mind putting muscle into it. Smaller Microplanes are good for citrus zest or grating nutmeg.

GINGER GRATER: This is a specialty tool, often circular or shaped like a fish. It grates ginger while also removing the stringy fiber and gathering the ginger juice.

FOR STEAMING

There are a few different ways to steam vegetables. My preference is a pot equipped for the job, often called a steamer or multi-cooker. It's constructed like a stockpot, with a shallow insert that holds the vegetables. The insert is filled with holes, so water can boil in the stockpot and steam the vegetables in the insert. Find a pot with a tightly fitting lid, so the steam can't escape.

You might also have a bamboo steamer that fits into a pot. That works well, too, with the downside that it takes up a bunch of space in the kitchen. Or you might have a collapsible metal insert, which I've found is fun for toddlers to play with when they're searching through the kitchen drawers, but cumbersome to use when steaming. In a pinch, simply fill a pot with 1 inch of water and add the vegetables directly to it. The bottoms of the veggies will get boiled, but the rest will steam.

FOR ROASTING

Invest in a few heavy-bottomed rimmed baking sheets. They won't buckle, and they'll cook everything more evenly. Many recipes in this book call for parchment paper for easy cleanup. This is different from waxed paper, which will melt in the oven.

FOR GRILLING

Any of the grilling recipes in this book will work with a gas or charcoal grill. Use your judgment when it comes to heat and timing; the heat can really vary, especially when you're working on a charcoal grill. If you don't have a grill or you don't want to fire it up, you can usually accomplish a similar effect by using the broiler setting of your oven.

BARELY
RECIPES

I COULD EAT THE MAJORITY OF VEGETABLES STEAMED WITH A LITTLE olive oil and tamari every day. It's just about the simplest way to prepare them, but still it might be the best. Broccoli, bok choy, Napa cabbage, watercress, kale—this is all they need. Five minutes in a steamer, olive oil, tamari. Bam.

Dig a little deeper into anyone's distaste for a particular vegetable, and you'll likely uncover an unfortunate preparation that lodged a taste in their memory. They hate Brussels sprouts because their dad used to boil them down to a mush. (And, oh, the smell that made in the house! Awful.) They refuse green beans because of the persistent presence of the slimy rubbery canned green bean on the dinner table all through childhood. They don't like kale because they've been faced with one too many chewy, jaw-busting kale salads. All it takes is one bad dish, and the vegetable gets a bad rap.

Luckily it's equally as easy to turn a negative opinion positive with a good dish. I've seen it happen again and again, heard those words: "I don't even like [fill in the blank], but I love this! What did you do?" Sometimes it's about knowing the little tricks to really bring out the best in a vegetable, but often it's about knowing when to leave it alone. This chapter has the simplest recipes in the book, but they're also the most essential. My hope is that each recipe is a lesson about the vegetable itself, a study in the essence of what makes that vegetable so good. These are the basics. Pull them out when simplicity is key, and the vegetable itself will do the impressing. Most of all, the central lesson vegetables have to offer is right here, on every page of this chapter: don't mess with a good thing.

CARAMELIZED HAKUREI TURNIPS

IT WAS THE HAKUREI TURNIP THAT GOT ME excited about new vegetables. These are not your thick-waisted Eastern European turnips. A Hakurei turnip is small, bright, and perishable like a radish, but sweet and earthy like a beet. Most of all, it is silky and almost creamy. It doesn't crunch. It is, hands down, the sexiest vegetable I know.

During my first year selling vegetables at the farmers' market, I had to learn how to talk about this strange white root. Conventional wisdom has us slicing them into salads (hence one of their alternate names: the salad turnip), but I'd recently discovered how amazing they became when I caramelized them in the oven. I created a whole lot of turnip converts that year. Hakurei turnips are also wonderful in soup with their greens (see page 87), or simply panfried in butter. The key is not to combine them with too many other ingredients; you need to push their flavor into the spotlight to really taste them. When you get home from the market, cut off the turnip greens and store them separately in a plastic bag in the refrigerator. They're tender and quick cooking, like spinach.

SERVES 4

2 tablespoons olive oil, plus more for greasing the baking sheet
2 bunches Hakurei turnips, greens removed, washed but not peeled
1 teaspoon kosher salt
Freshly ground black pepper

1. Preheat the oven to 425°F. Grease a baking sheet lightly with olive oil.

2. Slice the turnips about ¼ inch thick. You can do this with the slicing disk of a food processor, an adjustable mandoline, or a knife. Combine the turnips, the 2 tablespoons of olive oil, and salt in a large bowl, and toss gently to coat. Pile the turnips on the prepared baking sheet, spreading them in as close to a single layer as possible.

3. Roast the turnips until they crisp up and turn golden around the edges, 15 to 20 minutes. Shuffle the turnips and roast for 5 minutes more. Remove from the oven and top with freshly ground pepper.

ROASTED ASPARAGUS WITH YUMMY SAUCE

I PLANTED ASPARAGUS IN MY SEVENTH year of living in our house, and I ate my first spear in the tenth. It took me that long, because I needed to learn that my garden space and energy should be devoted to the foods I really wanted to eat and couldn't get for cheap. When organic local asparagus peaked at $8.99 a pound, I knew it was time.

Roasting is far and above my favorite way to cook asparagus. The insides steam and the outsides caramelize, and there are few more beautiful things to me than a baking sheet holding a chorus line of asparagus spears. They really don't need sauce, but a great sauce can't hurt, and yummy sauce might be the greatest I know. It made its first appearance with salmon in my book *The Homemade Kitchen,* but I just had to bring it back. The cheesy, ferment-y richness of nutritional yeast blends into a sauce with a flavor that everyone wants more of, yet no one can guess the main ingredient. Use it on sweet potatoes, squash, or green beans, too.

If you're buying asparagus at the supermarket, pay attention to the heads. If they've begun to open, or the feathered top is slimy, look for another bunch. Always wash asparagus well, as grit tends to hide in the feathered layers of each tip.

SERVES 4

1 teaspoon olive oil, plus more for greasing the baking sheet

1 pound asparagus

¼ teaspoon kosher salt

2 tablespoons unsalted butter

1½ teaspoons finely minced garlic (1 to 2 cloves)

1 tablespoon nutritional yeast

1½ teaspoons tamari or soy sauce

1. Preheat the oven to 425°F. Generously grease a baking sheet with olive oil.

2. Break the end of each asparagus stalk where it snaps naturally. (Compost the ends or save them for stock or asparagus soup.) Make sure the stalks are as dry as possible. Lay the stalks out on the baking sheet, and drizzle them with 1 teaspoon of olive oil. Sprinkle with the salt. Roast until the tips color, 10 to 12 minutes, shaking the pan halfway through roasting to turn the spears. Transfer the asparagus to a platter.

3. While the asparagus roast, make the sauce. Combine the butter, garlic, nutritional yeast, and tamari in your smallest saucepan over medium heat. Cook, stirring often, until the mixture comes together and thickens up into a sauce, 3 to 5 minutes. If it doesn't come together, add about a tablespoon of water and stir to combine. Pour the sauce over the asparagus or serve it on the side for dipping.

CREAMY SPINACH WITH DILL

CLASSIC CREAMED SPINACH IS GOOD IN A mashed-potatoes or mac-and-cheese kind of way—it's usually all cream and flour, with the spinach adding only color. This is a different dish, and that's why I call it *creamy,* not creamed, spinach. The cream's function here is to infuse with the garlic and nutmeg, and it adds just enough richness to elevate this above straight-up sautéed spinach. And the dill stands here as a green, too, combining with the spinach to make something like spanakopita in a bowl.

SERVES 4

1 tablespoon unsalted butter

¼ cup finely chopped onion

1 pound spinach, large stems removed, roughly chopped

⅓ cup heavy cream

1 garlic clove, pressed through a garlic press or crushed into a paste with the side of the knife

¼ teaspoon grated nutmeg, preferably fresh

¼ teaspoon kosher salt

Freshly ground black pepper

⅓ cup roughly chopped fresh dill

1. Melt the butter in a large pot set over medium heat. Add the onion and cook, stirring often, until soft and translucent, 3 to 5 minutes. Load the spinach into the pan, cover, and cook, stirring once or twice, until wilted, 2 to 3 minutes. Spoon the spinach and onions into a bowl, and drain and discard any liquid left in the pot. Return the pot to medium heat.

2. Pour the cream into the empty pot. Add the garlic and nutmeg. Let the cream come to a low simmer, and cook, stirring often, until it thickens and reduces slightly, 2 to 3 minutes. Stir in the salt and several grinds of pepper.

3. Give the spinach a squeeze to remove any excess liquid and return it to the pot, tossing to coat it in the reduced cream. Remove the pot from the heat and stir in the dill. Taste and add more salt or pepper, if necessary.

DILLY QUICK-PICKLED CUCUMBERS

I WILL HAPPILY EAT A CUCUMBER OF ANY quality or variety. I like to slice it, sprinkle with salt, and add a few drops of rice vinegar. This is my standard quick snack for unexpected visitors, and a plate of cucumbers given this treatment will always disappear, usually with requests to share my secret.

Occasionally a cucumber will be bitter, so always taste a slice first. If you've got a bitter cucumber, slice off one end and rub the flesh side of that nub gently against the flesh side of the rest of the cucumber in circles. You'll see liquid gather, releasing some of the bitterness of the cucumber. It doesn't entirely alleviate it, but it will make it edible.

I love smaller Persian cucumbers, which you often find packaged in Styrofoam at the supermarket. They're rarely bitter, and they have fewer seeds than your standard Kirby or English cucumber. If you're buying cukes from a farmer, look for varieties that don't look like cucumbers at all: lemon cucumbers, named as such not because they taste like lemons but because they are round with yellow, spiky skin; and sweet salt and pepper cucumbers that are white with tiny dark spikes.

This recipe is a cross between a salad and a condiment. Quick-pickling the cucumbers increases their crunch and longevity, and the salt brings out their sweetness and juice. Eat them alone, or scoop a bit on a salad, a bowl of rice, or a sandwich. A mandoline is helpful in the task of preparing these cucumbers.

MAKES ABOUT 2 CUPS

1 pound cucumbers, sliced paper thin
1½ teaspoons kosher salt
2 tablespoons finely chopped fresh dill
1½ tablespoons rice vinegar

1. Combine the cucumbers and salt in a colander. Gently massage the salt into the cucumbers, then let them drain for about 20 minutes.

2. Taste a cucumber. It should be salty, but not enough to make your mouth pucker. If the cucumbers are too salty, give them a light rinse under cold water to remove some of the salt. Transfer the cucumbers to a medium bowl, and fold in the dill and vinegar. Refrigerate for at least another 30 minutes before eating. Leftovers will keep in an airtight container in the refrigerator for up to 5 days.

COMPOUND
BUTTERS

I LOOK FOR RECIPES THAT GIVE ME A whole lot of fancy for minimal work, time, and money, and compound butters are the queens of this category. Butter goes well with just about everything, and when we mix delicious things into butter, it goes well *on* just about everything. Compound butters are also a great way to preserve fleeting and delicate herbs and petals, and they even freeze nicely. Experiment with any herbs or edible flowers you might have—you really can't mess this up. It seems (and, of course, this is true) that this recipe is just an excuse to spread the butter thicker on bread, but butter is also a good carrier for flavors. Chopped tarragon doesn't just sit in the softened butter; it infuses the whole thing with its delicate flavor. Nasturtium petals, usually prized not so much for their flavor but for the burst of red or orange they add to a salad, permeate butter with spice as well as color. Spread compound butters on bread or radishes (see page 235), or melt a pat over meat or fish. Of course, if you want to just eat them with a spoon, I won't judge.

MAKES ½ CUP

½ cup (1 stick) unsalted butter, at room temperature
½ teaspoon kosher salt
1 teaspoon fresh lemon juice
2 to 4 tablespoons chopped fresh herbs, edible flowers, shallots, garlic, minced radishes, or a mixture

Combine the butter, salt, lemon juice, and any additional ingredients in a medium bowl, mixing until well incorporated. Transfer to a ramekin, cover, and refrigerate until ready to use. The butter will keep in the refrigerator for up to a week. You can also shape the butter into a log, wrap it in plastic, and freeze for up to 6 months.

STEAMED BABY
BOK CHOY
WITH SESAME

BOK CHOY IS A TYPE OF CHINESE CABBAGE
especially adored in my house for its clean,
refreshing flavor and texture. It comes in big
and little sizes, and while the big version is
great chopped and stir-fried, I love to steam
the babies. They're so pleasing all tucked into
the steamer together, and steaming the whole
heads preserves the juiciness I especially love
about this vegetable. Baby bok choy heads can
also be cut in half and roasted—this keeps
the hearts juicy but increases the crisp of the
leaves. Just halve them, rub with oil, and roast
in a 450°F oven for 15 minutes.

SERVES 4

6 heads baby bok choy
2 tablespoons sesame seeds
1 tablespoon Asian sesame oil
2 teaspoons tamari or soy sauce

1. Separate the levels of your steamer pot.
Fill the lower level with a few inches of water
and set the pot over high heat to bring the
water to a boil. Tuck the bok choy heads into
the upper level of the steamer in as close to
a single layer as possible. (If your babies are
big, you can also cut them in half lengthwise.)
Insert the upper level into the lower and cover
the pot. Steam until the heads are bright
green and tender, 6 to 8 minutes.

2. While the bok choy steams, prepare the
sauce. Heat a small skillet or saucepan set
over medium heat. Toast the sesame seeds in
the skillet, stirring frequently, until they color
and begin to pop, 2 to 3 minutes. Add the
sesame oil and tamari, and heat just until the
sauce is warmed through, 1 to 2 minutes.

3. Use tongs to carefully transfer the bok
choy heads to a wide serving bowl, shaking
each head in the pot to drain the excess water.
Spoon the seeds and sauce over the bok choy.

ROASTED BEETS, JULIA-STYLE

"HAVE I EVER TOLD YOU ABOUT THE DAY Julia Child stopped in front of my garden, got out of the car, and schooled me on the *only* way to cook a beet?"

My friend Jane's garden isn't grand or perfectly manicured; in fact, it's small and wild within the four walls of the handmade fence, and it fed her family for decades. It's one of my favorite gardens, and I'm not alone. Because, apparently, Julia Child was visiting friends in the Berkshires who had been to Jane's garden, and they thought she just had to see it. And that's how Jane got schooled by Julia in the middle of her beet patch.

"The only way to cook a beet," Jane told me in her perfect Julia voice, "is in a covered roasting pan in a very hot oven. Douse it with a little olive oil, balsamic vinegar, and a splash of red wine. It will be done in a jiff, and absolutely *glorious*." This is the only way Jane cooks her beets, and I can confirm from experience that it does create a glorious beet. I'll add the wine if I have a bottle open, but I find the balsamic really is the essential element.

I love everything about beets—their color, earthiness, sugar, and versatility. I often cook two bunches at a time, and leftovers become an ingredient to enjoy throughout the week. Use them in Beet and Cucumber Quinoa (page 124). And if you buy your beets with greens, save them for Miso Greens (page 40) or Polenta with All the Greens (page 166). Try, if you can, to use beets of a similar size, so that they'll all take about the same time to cook.

SERVES 4

1½ pounds beets (3 to 5 medium beets), 1 inch of tops and tails attached
1 tablespoon balsamic vinegar
1 tablespoon olive oil, plus more as needed
Optional: 2 tablespoons red wine
Kosher salt

1. Preheat the oven to 450°F.

2. Wash the beets and nestle them into a roasting pan. Drizzle with the balsamic vinegar, 1 tablespoon of olive oil, and wine, if using. Cover the pan with a tight-fitting lid or aluminum foil. Roast until tender when pricked with a fork, 40 to 60 minutes, depending on the size of the beets. Remove the pan from the oven and carefully lift the lid or foil. Let the beets cool until you can comfortably touch them.

3. Use your hands or a paring knife to remove the top and tail of each beet. Then apply pressure to the skin and slide it right off. If the beets are cooked enough, the skin should come off easily. If it doesn't, use a paring knife. If you're making the beets to use later, store them whole in a covered container in the refrigerator. To use right away, chop each beet into bite-sized pieces and place them in a serving bowl. Add a sprinkle of salt and, if they seem to need it, a glug of olive oil.

TIP If you've made beets for dinner, everyone knows it from your red-stained hands. The stains will fade in a day, but to remove them right away, rub your hands with coarse salt under cold water.

GREEN BEANS WITH ALMONDS AND BROWN BUTTER

MY FAVORITE KIND OF GREEN BEAN IS NOT green at all but pale yellow streaked with purple, appropriately called Dragon's Lingerie. It's always been one of the beans the farm I work for grows and sells at the market, and I never miss a chance to say it out loud when they're for sale. There's nothing like making a buttoned-up New Englander blush with the mention of underwear, especially when you're talking about something as mundane as a bean. There are other varieties, too: a skinny dark purple bean the color of eggplant, bright yellow wax beans, traditional green haricots verts. And why are these all "green" beans? The name refers not to the color, but to the maturity. All green beans, no matter their color, are in fact young beans.

For years I blanched my beans and tossed them in butter. But then I came across this method, brought into print by Food52's *Genius Recipes*, written by Kristen Miglore. There's no water involved, and the beans get crispy and crunchy around the edges and incredibly creamy in the middle. She adds garlic right at the end of cooking, a delicious way to finish them. Here I go traditional with a little browned butter and a handful of toasted almonds. They're as good on an ordinary quick summer dinner table as they are on a Thanksgiving spread. If you're buying your beans in the store, they're probably green, and that's okay, too. Gather the beans in a handful and slice off their tops and tails. If your beans are fresher or you picked them yourself, just top them. You can leave the tail end on.

SERVES 4

2½ tablespoons unsalted butter
1 pound green beans (any variety or any color)
½ lemon
¼ cup sliced or roughly chopped almonds
½ teaspoon large flake sea salt, such as Maldon

1. Melt 1 tablespoon of the butter in a large skillet set over medium-high heat. Add the beans and cook, stirring frequently, until they color and blister in spots, about 5 minutes. Reduce the heat to medium-low, cover the skillet, and continue to cook, stirring and peeking in on them every so often, until the beans are tender, 8 to 10 minutes. Transfer the beans to a serving bowl and return the skillet to medium heat. Gently squeeze the lemon over the beans.

2. Melt the remaining 1½ tablespoons of butter over medium heat in the same skillet. Continue to heat it, keeping a close eye on the pan, until the butter turns golden and smells nutty, 2 to 5 minutes. Pour the butter over the beans and return the skillet to the heat. Toast the almonds in the pan, shuffling constantly, until a few almonds show color, 1 to 2 minutes. Pour the almonds over the beans and sprinkle with the large flake salt.

MISO GREENS

MISO SOUP WAS SICK FOOD IN MY HOUSE when I was a kid, so there was always a container of miso in the fridge. It can be an intimidating ingredient—thick, salty, and seemingly expensive. But it lasts nearly forever in the refrigerator, and when it comes to vegetables, miso should be a standard ingredient. Varieties range from white miso, which is very mellow in flavor, to red miso, which is much stronger and earthier. All varieties are made according to Japanese tradition, starting with rice, barley, or another grain that's first fermented and then combined with cooked beans (usually soy) to ferment again. The result is a densely flavored, thick paste that adds a wonderful saltiness to anything. And because it's fermented, miso is a live food, as good for your body as it is for the flavor of your recipe. Like all live foods, miso shouldn't be boiled. You want to keep all those good organisms alive! These days you can find all sorts of miso in an Asian grocery or natural foods store.

This is a great simple treatment for any hearty green. If you've bought root vegetables with their tops, save the greens and cook them all together.

SERVES 4

2 tablespoons unsalted butter
2 large bunches (8 to 10 ounces each) any hearty green (kale, kohlrabi, broccoli greens, collards, Swiss chard, etc.), stemmed if necessary, roughly chopped
½ cup water
3 tablespoons white or red miso paste
1 garlic clove, pressed or finely minced

1. Heat a large skillet or wide sauté pan over medium heat. Melt the butter in the skillet and continue to heat it until it foams up and then clears again, 2 to 3 minutes. Add the greens and water, and increase the heat to medium-high. Cover the pan and let cook, stirring once or twice, until the greens begin to wilt, 3 to 4 minutes. Take the pan off the heat.

2. Using a spoon to hold back the greens, pour most of the pan liquid into a small bowl. Measure the miso into a separate small bowl and add a splash of the greens' cooking liquid. Stir and repeat until you have a thin paste. Add the miso mixture back to the pan, along with the garlic. Put the pan back over medium-low heat and cook, stirring frequently, until the miso mixture coats the greens, another 2 to 3 minutes.

STEAMED GRILLED CORN WITH THREE SAUCES

IN MY PART OF THE WORLD, CORN IS FOR August and the first bit of September. When I was little, my grandmother would swing by Taft Farms in Great Barrington, Massachusetts, on our way home from this or that errand, and I'd nearly fall into the great vats in front of the store as I picked out our ears. A dozen ears are too much for one meal, but we'd buy that many anyway, because when the price is listed by the dozen it's just an excuse to eat more corn. She used to *tsk, tsk* at the people before us who had opened each ear, looking for perfect worm-free kernels, and now I never check.

There are plenty of ways to prepare corn perfectly when it's in season. Convention tells us to boil it, and I think everyone would agree that's perfectly acceptable. I only boiled corn until I was an adult, and I never felt like I was missing anything. Opinions get more heated when it comes to grilling corn. Husk on? Husk off? Do we do all the work for the eater and remove the silk before wrapping it back up in the husk? And then there's the soak. How long? And in what? I grill corn if the grill is hot and convenient, I keep the corn in its husk so that it steams inside its own envelope. This way, the kernels are sweet and plump and uncharred. I like to add a little vinegar and salt to the soak, because I've found that makes the ears juicier. And although butter is really the only condiment you need, I've included a few optional additions that always work out well.

MAKES 6 EARS

¼ cup red wine vinegar
1 tablespoon kosher salt
6 ears of corn, husks on

1. Fill a tub, bucket, or your sink with cold water. Stir in the vinegar and salt, and add the corn (with husks on). Soak for 20 minutes.

2. Meanwhile, heat your grill until it's quite hot.

3. Drain the corn and transfer it to the grates of the hot grill. Cook, turning regularly, for 10 to 12 minutes. Pull back a section of the husk and test for doneness. The kernels should be bright and glossy; blow on the ear and take a bite. If it's sweet and wonderful, remove the other ears from the grill; otherwise give them another 2 to 3 minutes.

AND THREE SAUCES

MINT BUTTER: Finely chop a handful of fresh mint leaves and combine them with ¼ cup (½ stick) of room-temperature unsalted butter and ¼ teaspoon salt. Slather over each ear.

SPICY STREET CORN: Combine 2 tablespoons mayonnaise with ¼ cup sour cream. Stir in ½ cup of crumbled feta or Cotija cheese, ½ teaspoon finely chopped garlic, and ½ to 1 teaspoon ancho chile powder. Fold in ¼ cup of chopped cilantro, if you're a cilantro lover. Squeeze fresh lime juice over each ear as you eat it.

SAGE BROWN BUTTER: Melt ¼ cup (½ stick) unsalted butter in a small saucepan over medium heat. When the foam subsides and the butter turns slightly brown, add 10 fresh sage leaves. Remove the pan from the heat, and as the sage leaves begin to curl, transfer them to a paper-towel-lined plate. Paint the corn with the browned butter, and crumble the sage leaves over each ear.

CARAMELIZED CORN WITH MINT

THERE ARE SO MANY WAYS TO ENJOY FRESH, perfectly-at-peak produce, but the recipes that make the most of frozen or out-of-season produce can be especially helpful. I came upon this method in Julia Moskin's *New York Times* column during the dead of winter, when all I had in the fridge was some limp, well-traveled broccoli and a few ancient beets. I did, however, have corn in the freezer, usually reserved for Corn Chowder (page 96) or shepherd's pie. The corn—added to hot butter until it browns and pops in the pan—becomes sweet and caramelized. The mint makes it all taste like summer, even in February, so even if you're not a mint lover, give it a try anyway.

SERVES 2 TO 3

3 tablespoons unsalted butter
1 10-ounce bag frozen corn or 2 cups fresh (from 3 to 4 ears)
¼ cup roughly chopped fresh mint
½ teaspoon kosher salt

Melt the butter in a cast-iron skillet or enameled Dutch oven set over medium-high heat. Add the corn and cook, stirring occasionally, until it caramelizes and turns golden, 10 to 15 minutes. Remove the pan from the heat, stir in the mint, and sprinkle with salt.

FROZEN VEGETABLES

Frozen vegetables have gotten a bad rap with the whole local/seasonal movement, but it's just not fair. There are certain vegetables that I find to be totally undelicious when reheated from frozen, but others freeze beautifully and cook up nearly as bright as the day they were picked. Frozen peas will enliven everything from stove-top mac and cheese to Indian Spiced Shepherd's Pie (page 208), and frozen corn makes great Corn Chowder (page 96). The key is to barely cook them at all beyond the state you found them in. Just defrost under cold running water, or add frozen to whatever you're cooking.

You can freeze your own vegetables, too. I never come into a wealth of shelling peas magnificent enough to actually freeze them, but if you do, all they need is a quick blanch before freezing. Lay the blanched peas out on a tray to freeze before bagging them—if you're a perfectionist—or just throw them into bags if you don't mind giving the bag a whack on the counter when you pull it back out. Corn is a great vegetable to freeze yourself as well. Enlist a few family members and get an assembly line going. Remove the husks, cook the corn for a minute, and dunk the cobs in a bucket of ice water. Then use a knife to remove the kernels. Transfer the kernels to bags, pat them flat so they lie in a neat stack, and freeze.

For greens, follow the same method as above—boiling water, ice water, freezer bags. The greens aren't wonderful on their own, but a brick cooked into Kale and White Bean Soup with Rosemary Oil (page 108) is just as good as the real, fresh thing.

BOILED NEW POTATOES WITH SALSA VERDE

NEW POTATOES ARE NOT SIMPLY LITTLE fancy potatoes; they are actually potatoes dug and harvested before they are fully mature. If you scrape a potato with your nail and the skin comes right off, you have a new potato in your hands. When we grow potatoes at home, we are so excited about eating them that we end up consuming all new potatoes and no mature ones. What makes a new potato different from your average one is that it has a creaminess and delicate flavor you won't find in a mature potato and it should be used within a few days. I tend to boil or steam new potatoes, since gentle cooking keeps the texture really creamy and gives the flavor a chance to come through. I love them with a good herby sauce like this one, as the punchiness of the anchovies and capers really enhances the flavor of the potato. (Of course, if you've got more mature potatoes, this sauce will do nicely for them, too.) This recipe is good at any temperature, but I like it best slightly warm or at room temperature.

SERVES 4 TO 6

2 pounds new potatoes, peeled or not, cut into 1½-inch chunks
Kosher salt
¼ cup chopped fresh basil
¼ cup chopped fresh flat-leaf parsley
1 teaspoon finely minced garlic (1 clove)
5 anchovies, rinsed and finely minced
1 tablespoon capers, roughly chopped
¼ cup extra-virgin olive oil

1. Put the potatoes in a large stockpot and cover them with several inches of cold water. Add about ½ teaspoon of salt to the pot, cover it, and bring the water and potatoes to a boil over high heat. Reduce the heat to medium-high, uncover the pot, and cook until the potatoes are tender when stabbed with a fork, 10 to 15 minutes. Drain the potatoes in a colander.

2. While the potatoes cook, make the salsa verde. Combine the basil, parsley, garlic, anchovies, and capers in the bottom of a large bowl. Stir in the olive oil.

3. Add the potatoes to the sauce, tossing to coat them. Season with salt.

ROASTED POTATOES

MY FRIEND FLAVIO MAKES THE BEST roasted potatoes. I ate them for years and felt a little bad about myself, puzzled as to why I, too, couldn't instinctively master such a simple and delicious dish. Mine were good, but they just didn't have the crispy outside and creamy inside like Flavio's. His didn't seem to have any secret ingredients, and I assumed he just knew his way around a potato better than I did. Finally, I asked. His secret was that he cooks them twice: first in the steamer and then in the oven. The steam actually cooks the potatoes, and the oven crisps them. This method works well with any kind of potato, and you can peel or not, depending on your preference.

SERVES 4 TO 6

2 pounds potatoes, cut into 1½-inch chunks
2 tablespoons olive oil, plus more for greasing the baking sheet
Kosher salt

1. Separate the levels of your steamer pot. Fill the lower level with a few inches of water and set the pot over high heat to bring the water to a boil. Put the potatoes in the upper level of the steamer. Insert the upper level into the lower and cover the pot. Steam until the potatoes are just tender when stabbed with a fork, about 10 minutes.

2. Meanwhile, preheat the oven to 475°F. Grease a rimmed baking sheet with oil.

3. Transfer the potatoes from the steamer to the prepared baking sheet. Drizzle with the olive oil and sprinkle with salt. Roast until the potatoes are golden brown and crispy around the edges, about 25 minutes. Remove the baking sheet from the oven, taste a potato (carefully!), and add more salt, if needed.

SWEET AND SPICY COLLARD GREENS

COLLARD RECIPES TEND TO INVOLVE hours and hours of cooking the greens in vinegar and bacon fat. The result is delicious, both sour and rich, and for many, that's just what collard greens need to be. But collards are like any other hearty green, and there's nothing inherently in them that requires all that cooking. Cook collards for just a few minutes, and they retain their texture, which is smooth and strong and satisfying. They do respond well to fat, and I love to cook them with butter. I add a splash of vinegar and a bit of garlic, and it brings just enough of that classic cooked-all-day collard flavor, while still keeping it all fresh and green.

SERVES 4

1 large bunch collards, thicker stems removed and leaves cut into thin ribbons
2 tablespoons unsalted butter
¼ cup water
¼ teaspoon kosher salt
1 teaspoon finely minced garlic (1 clove)
1½ tablespoons apple cider vinegar
Freshly ground black pepper

Combine the collards, butter, and water in a wide saucepan set over medium-high heat. Cover the pan and bring the water up to a boil. Reduce the heat to medium and cook, stirring occasionally, until the greens are tender and wilted, 5 to 8 minutes. Uncover the pan, add the salt, and cook, stirring often, until the water evaporates, 1 to 2 minutes. Remove the pan from the heat, and stir in the garlic, vinegar, and black pepper.

ROASTED BROCCOLI WITH LEMON AND PARMESAN

ROASTING BROCCOLI CREATES AN ENTIRELY different experience than steaming it. I like to leave it in larger "trees" to roast, mostly because the end result is so good that it becomes finger food. The stems stay firm and snappy, and the heads of the trees char just enough to create a tiny crunch.

Pre-salting the broccoli is a trick I learned from my mother. She works at a farm with a great kitchen, and one of the cooks had made "the best broccoli" my mom had eaten in a long time. She pulled the secret from him, so she could share it with me. The 20 minutes between salting and roasting draws extra moisture from the broccoli, and this creates an incredibly tender tree that caramelizes but doesn't burn.

SERVES 3 TO 4

1 pound broccoli, stems trimmed, cut into tall trees
¾ teaspoon kosher salt
1½ tablespoons olive oil
1 teaspoon fresh lemon juice
¼ cup finely grated Parmesan cheese

1. Put the broccoli in a colander and sprinkle with the salt, massaging the florets a bit to get the most salt-to-broccoli contact. Let it sit for 20 minutes.

2. Meanwhile, preheat the oven to 350°F.

3. Transfer the broccoli to a baking sheet, dabbing it with a paper towel or clean dish towel to remove any liquid as you go. Drizzle with the olive oil and gently stir to coat the broccoli.

4. Roast the broccoli until the stems are tender and the tree heads are crispy, about 25 minutes. Transfer the broccoli to a serving bowl, add the lemon juice and Parmesan, and toss to combine.

CHEESY
BROCCOLI

WHEN I WAS LITTLE AND LOVED BROC-
coli more than any other food except cold
cereal or buttered noodles, my grandfather
would make me "cheesy broccoli." My grandparents both disapproved of my pickiness but
couldn't bear to see me go without greens, so
the house was stocked with broccoli every
time I arrived. And because they were my
grandparents and had to find little ways to
spoil me, my grandfather would always give
into my requests for extra cheese. The cheese
would melt and bubble, and it was more delicious than anything: tender and green below,
but tangy and cheesy above.

I remembered the simple trick of cheesy
broccoli years into my parenting life, when
enough time had gone by that it seemed like
a new idea. Now it's on the birthday and
sleepover rotation, not because it's labor- or
time-intensive, but because I like to hold on
to the recipe for little celebrations.

For non-cheesy normal weeknight broccoli, I steam the florets and drizzle them with
olive oil. But when we need it to be special, it's
all about the cheese.

SERVES 4

1 pound broccoli
1½ cups grated Cheddar cheese

1. Separate the levels of your steamer pot. Fill
the lower level with a few inches of water, and
set the pot over high heat to bring the water
to a boil.

2. While the water boils, prepare the broccoli.
Cut off the main stem and trim away the
scarred bottom. Slice the stem into ½-inch
rounds. Then separate the broccoli head into
florets, slicing first through the remaining
stem, then moving on to slice through each
head to create 2- to 3-inch florets.

3. Preheat the broiler to 450°F or medium-
high, depending on your options.

4. Pack the broccoli into the upper level of
the steamer basket. Insert the upper level
into the lower level and cover the pot. Steam
until the florets are tender and don't taste
grassy, 5 to 7 minutes.

5. Transfer to a 9 × 13-inch broiler-proof
baking pan and top with the grated cheese.
Broil until the cheese melts and becomes
crispy, 1 to 2 minutes.

A BIG BOWL
OF KALE

KALE HAS RISEN AND FALLEN WITH THE trends, but it's always been a great green. It's easy to grow, cheap to buy, and versatile. It's mellow and hearty enough to go into soups, but tasty and delicate enough to eat on its own.

There are several varieties of kale, and they're quite different from one another. Curly kale is the most typical, frilly and hearty with a tough stem. Lacinato kale (also known as Tuscan kale or *cavolo nero*) leaves are long, thin, and much more delicate than curly kale leaves. They have a bumpy texture that earns the nickname "dinosaur kale," and often the stems are tender enough to eat with the leaves. You might also see Red Russian kale, similar in appearance to curly but with a flatter leaf and a purple tinge around the edges. Each variety has its own taste and texture, and curly and Red Russian tend to lend themselves better to long cooking than Lacinato.

Like broccoli, kale is best when it gets the tamari and olive oil treatment, as in this recipe. Start with a bunch of kale—any variety. Wash it well by filling a sink or large bowl with water, adding a splash of white vinegar, and submerging the kale in the water. Swish it around a bit, then transfer it to a dish towel on the counter. Kale stems are usually thick and woody, so unless you're working with very tender Lacinato, it's best to eat the leaves and save the stems for stock. To remove the leaves from the stems, grasp a stem at its base, and run your hand up the stem, separating the leaf as you go.

SERVES 4

1 large bunch kale (about 8 ounces), stemmed and torn or cut into bite-sized pieces
½ teaspoon tamari or soy sauce, plus more as needed
2 teaspoons olive oil

1. Separate the levels of your steamer pot. Fill the lower level with a few inches of water and set the pot over high heat to bring the water to a boil. Pack the kale into the upper level of the steamer. Steam until the kale is silky and doesn't resist your teeth at all. This will take about 4 minutes for Lacinato kale, and a few more for curly or Red Russian.

2. Dump the steamed kale into a bowl, and top with the tamari and olive oil. Toss to coat the leaves; taste and add more tamari if necessary.

KALE AFTER THE FROST

Kale is a cruciferous vegetable, which puts it in a family with cabbage, broccoli, and cauliflower. It is a cold-weather vegetable that grows and thrives beyond the usual hot summer window of growing seasons. These vegetables are hearty and travel well, and they're always available at the average grocery store.

Most grocery-store kale—like grocery-store anything in the United States—is from California. It's good and inexpensive, and conventional kale doesn't tend to be sprayed too heavily with pesticides. I often opt to buy conventionally grown kale, as organic kale in the grocery store can be withered and bunched into a small measly amount, whereas a bunch of conventional kale will feed my family through a few dinners for three bucks. All in all, it's a decent vegetable to choose when you're standing in the produce aisle at the supermarket.

But I strongly recommend you try to find local kale picked after the first frost. It may sound like a stretch to call kale a delicacy, but November garden kale grown in colder climates is just that. That special kale has been through a frost, and the result is a leaf that's not only more tender but far sweeter. If you've ever made a judgment between a summer tomato and one you might encounter in the supermarket in January, you'll find a similar comparison in the seasons of kale. I'm not kidding about the frost, either. Some of the best kale of the year comes in the early winter, when the leaves are half frozen and holding snow in their crevices.

Unfortunately, it's hard to find kale that's been through a frost. If you live in a colder climate, your best bet is to grow it, and even if you have a tiny space or limited garden experience, a few kale plants are a great place to start. If you can't grow it yourself, seek it out at fall and winter farmers' markets. And if you live in a warm climate, you're out of luck. (Now you know how New Englanders feel when you talk about your citrus trees.) But someday take a vacation to New England in December, and make sure you put kale on your itinerary.

KALE SALAD

ALTHOUGH I PREFER TO COOK MY KALE, I do like a nice raw kale salad when it's done right. Kale tends to be decent year-round, which I cannot say for the sad and withered lettuces that crowd into the spray case at the supermarket during our winter months. Kale doesn't get slimy under dressing, which means that you can make kale salad up to a day ahead of time, and it will be even more delicious than it was in its first hour. Because kale leaves are sturdier than lettuce, they also hold cheese or nuts or other delicious bits much better than lettuce. And when it comes down to it, a well-made kale salad is so good—it's the kind of dish that makes people stop in their tracks and beg for the recipe. In fact, that's what I did when I ate this version at my friend Lissa's table years ago.

The key is to cut your leaves super thin, to massage the kale to break it down, and to make sure the whole bowl of it sits for a bit before you dig in. I like to make this particular salad with curly kale, but any other variety will do as well.

SERVES 4

1 bunch kale (7 to 8 ounces), stemmed, washed, and dried
1½ tablespoons fresh lemon juice
1½ tablespoons rice vinegar or red wine vinegar
1½ tablespoons olive oil
1 teaspoon finely minced garlic (1 clove)
1 tablespoon finely chopped preserved lemon rind (from ¼ preserved lemon; see page 57) or 1 teaspoon lemon zest
Kosher salt
Freshly ground black pepper
½ cup finely grated Parmesan cheese (about 1½ ounces)

1. Roll a few kale leaves together into a log and slice them as finely as possible. Repeat with the remaining leaves and put all the chopped kale in a medium bowl. Use both hands to massage the kale, breaking it down until it wilts under your hands. Don't be gentle, as the massage helps to make it more tender.

2. Combine the lemon juice, vinegar, olive oil, garlic, preserved lemon rind, ¼ teaspoon salt, and several grinds of pepper in a small jar. Shake vigorously and pour the dressing over the kale. Use a large fork to press the greens down, massaging the dressing in. Add the cheese, and massage or stir to distribute the cheese throughout the salad. Let it sit at room temperature for at least 20 minutes. Taste, and add more salt or pepper if necessary.

HOW TO MAKE
PRESERVED LEMONS

Preserved lemons are a staple in my kitchen, and they are used in many recipes in this book. They impart saltiness, sourness, and a general complexity to everything from salad dressings to chicken soup. You can buy preserved lemons at a specialty store, but they're easy to make at home.

To make a quart of lemons, you'll need about 1½ pounds organic lemons, ½ cup kosher salt, and 1 cup bottled lemon juice without any additives. For each lemon, cut off the bottom tip. Then cut the lemon lengthwise, leaving the stem end intact. Cut again lengthwise at a 90-degree angle to the first cut. The lemons should be quartered, but still attached at the stem end. Measure the salt into a bowl, and put the lemons into the salt, a few at a time, packing the salt into the cuts. Put the lemons into a sterilized quart-size jar, gently crushing them to help release their juice as you go. Layer salt from the bowl between the lemons, so that by the time the jar is filled, all the salt is in the jar. Finally, top off the jar with the bottled lemon juice, covering the top lemon. Cover the jar, give it a good shake to help dissolve the salt, and set it in your kitchen, out of direct sunlight, at room temperature. Let the jar ferment for 3 weeks, turning the jar over every so often to make sure the salt is able to cure all the lemons. Transfer the jar to the refrigerator, and eat the lemons within a year.

KOHLRABI FRIES

A BUNCH OF KOHLRABI LOOKS LIKE A TINY fleet of UFOs, and that's not even the strangest thing about it. The plant follows the same structural pattern as a root vegetable—bulb, stem, leaf—but it's not a root vegetable at all. The kohlrabi bulb grows *above* the ground, bulb perched on the soil, because it's actually in the cabbage family. And, in truth, the bulb is not a bulb but a swollen stem with an outer layer that has to be peeled off with a paring knife. It can be green or purple, and once you've cut your way through the skin, you'll find the white flesh to be sweet and crisp like an apple, starchy and earthy like a potato. You can slice this globe and eat it raw, using it as a vehicle for Caramelized Onion Dip (page 246) or some other delicious thing. You can also slice it into matchsticks and turn it into a slaw, where it will contribute all the good things about an apple without the browning or possible mealiness over time. I love kohlrabi braised, stewed, or steamed, but my favorite way to cook it is in the oven like fries, crispy and sweet on the outside, and creamy and tart on the inside.

Although you don't use them in this recipe, be sure to save your kohlrabi greens. They're hearty like collards, with the rich sweetness of broccoli greens. Use them in Miso Greens (page 40) or Polenta with All the Greens (page 166).

SERVES 3 TO 4

2 tablespoons olive oil, plus more for greasing the baking sheet
1 bunch kohlrabi (about 4 bulbs), purple or green, greens removed
Kosher salt

1. Preheat the oven to 425°F. Grease a baking sheet with olive oil.

2. Use a paring knife to peel the thick outer layer off each bulb until you have white orbs of kohlrabi. Slice each bulb into rough fry-like pieces, and put them into a bowl. Add the olive oil and ½ teaspoon salt, stirring to coat the vegetables. Spread them onto the prepared baking sheet. Bake until golden and tender, 35 to 40 minutes. Serve hot, with a bit more salt to taste.

THE
SIMPLEST SLAW

CABBAGE IS A VEGETABLE THAT STORES well, which means we can have decent cabbage throughout the fall and spring. That cabbage might show a bit of wear, but it's perfect for Caramelized Cabbage Soup (page 100), Braised Kabocha Squash with Miso and Purple Cabbage (page 197), or Butter-Braised Cabbage (page 62). But this recipe is for fresh cabbage that hasn't seen the inside of a root cellar. Maybe you grew it yourself or you picked out a light-green, weighty head at the market. Really fresh cabbage is so sweet and tender that you almost don't want to do anything to it at all.

I first had this slaw with my friends Michaele and Johannes. They made this slaw to go with cheeseburgers, and it quickly became the star of the table. What was the secret? "Good cabbage," Michaele said with a shrug. "Picked today." The other secret, it turns out, is to massage the cabbage really well. The more you get into it, the more the walls of the cabbage break down, and that produces an incredibly tender bite. I like this best with green cabbage, but the method will work well with red cabbage, too. Serve it over burgers, on pulled pork, or all by itself. And it just gets better with time, so feel free to make this one up to 2 days ahead.

SERVES 6

½ medium head green cabbage
(about 1 pound), cored, quartered, and
thinly sliced
Kosher salt
1 teaspoon finely minced garlic (1 clove)
1½ tablespoons olive oil

Put the cabbage in a medium bowl and sprinkle with ½ teaspoon salt. Use your hands to roughly massage the salt into the cabbage. Keep massaging until the cabbage shrinks and begins to release liquid, about 30 seconds. Stir in the garlic and olive oil, and let the slaw sit for about 5 minutes. Taste and add more salt, if necessary.

HOT SESAME CELERY WITH RUBY CABBAGE

CELERY IS AN EXCELLENT SUPPORTING character. It's easy to find, cheap to buy, and always reliable. But giving it a chance to shine can be hard. This quick little side dish changes that, putting the celery at the front and shoving the cabbage into the background. It's spicy and salty and has all the great flavors of a spring roll without the wrapper. I love this over rice with a little grilled chicken or tofu—with mellower foods, the celery and cabbage become almost a condiment. This is also a great filling for Scallion Crepes (page 216). It uses two kinds of sesame oil: Asian sesame oil and spicy sesame oil, which is often available in a small bottle from specialty stores. If you can't find the spicy oil, just omit it and add a pinch of crushed red pepper flakes to the dish instead.

SERVES 6

¼ cup sesame seeds

1½ tablespoons Asian sesame oil

3 stalks celery, thinly sliced

⅓ small head of purple cabbage
(8 to 10 ounces), halved and thinly sliced

1½ teaspoons tamari or soy sauce

¼ teaspoon spicy sesame oil

1. Heat a large, dry skillet over medium heat. Toast the sesame seeds in the skillet, shuffling them to keep them from burning, until they color slightly, 3 to 4 minutes. Transfer the seeds to a small bowl and return the pan to the heat.

2. Heat the sesame oil in the pan over medium heat until it shimmers, about 20 seconds. Add the celery and cook, stirring often, until it's soft, 3 to 4 minutes. Add the cabbage to the pan and toss with the celery. Cook, stirring often, until the cabbage is wilted and tender, 5 to 7 minutes. Remove the pan from the heat, and transfer the celery and cabbage to a serving bowl. Toss with the tamari, spicy sesame oil, and toasted sesame seeds.

BUTTER-BRAISED CABBAGE

A QUICK SCAN OF THIS BOOK'S RECIPE LIST will reveal my deep love for cabbage, and this is the recipe that started the whole affair. Alice Waters told me to throw it in a covered pan with an inch of water and a knob of butter, and, one night, desperate to make a dinner out of a weathered half head of cabbage in my fridge, I followed her advice. It plumped up and became creamy and sweet, and the quick braise in butter transformed the cabbage into a dish that was hard not to finish right out of the pan. One of my standard winter meals is a roast chicken, a pot of creamy polenta, and a side of buttered cabbage. It's a perfect trio.

Cabbage is a good vegetable to love. It's widely available through the year, inexpensive, and tends to overcome any age or quality challenges to come out delicious anyway. My favorite variety is the saucer-shaped light green cabbage called Tendersweet. It is exactly as its name describes, and it's usually the cabbage I grow if I can. But this recipe is great with any firm red or green cabbage, too, though the softer frilly cabbages like Napa or Savoy lend themselves more to steaming or coleslaw (see page 132). I recommend trying this inch-of-water-knob-of-butter-cover-the pot treatment with sturdy greens, too, especially broccoli raab and escarole. Just reduce the cooking time to 5 minutes.

SERVES 6

½ medium head of red or green cabbage (about 1 pound), cored, quartered, and roughly chopped
2 tablespoons unsalted butter
Kosher salt

Put the cabbage into a wide skillet or sauté pan, and add about an inch of water. Set the pan over medium-high heat, bring the water to a boil, and add the butter. Reduce the heat to medium-low to simmer the liquid, and cover the pan. Cook, stirring occasionally, until the cabbage is sweet and tender, 10 to 12 minutes. Uncover the pan, increase the heat to medium, and continue to stir. Sprinkle generously with salt and serve with any liquid from the pan.

PERFECT ROASTED CAULIFLOWER

ROASTED CAULIFLOWER DONE RIGHT IS crispy and caramelized on the outside and creamy on the inside. The mellow neutral nature of the cauliflower makes it an ideal base for every flavor from capers to tomatoes to cheese, though here I keep it simple with my favorite addition: cumin seed. Sometimes I have to roast two heads at once, since one tray disappears before dinner as everyone passes through the kitchen.

Cauliflower can get a bit moldy on the edges, and you might see a bit of black when you release it from its wrapper. That's okay—just trim those bits off and use the rest. And, especially at the farmers' market, you can find all sorts of cauliflower varieties that barely resemble the white standard. Purple, yellow, and the spiky lime-green Romanesco varieties are all wonderful prepared this way. Cauliflower cores don't roast up well, so if you're a scrap saver, hold on to them to bulk up soups or stocks. And although you might be tempted to save dishwashing time by using parchment here, resist the urge. The direct contact with the baking sheet is what creates the most delicious parts of each piece.

SERVES 4

1 tablespoon olive oil, plus more for greasing the baking sheet
1 large head cauliflower (about 2 pounds), cored and cut into small florets
Kosher salt
1 teaspoon cumin seeds

1. Preheat the oven to 425°F. Lightly grease a baking sheet with olive oil.

2. Combine the cauliflower, the 1 tablespoon of olive oil, 1 teaspoon salt, and the cumin seeds in a large bowl. Stir to coat the cauliflower, and then scrape the cauliflower onto the prepared baking sheet, taking care to bring any oil or seeds in the bowl with it. Use your hands to make sure the seeds are evenly dispersed over the cauliflower florets.

3. Roast until lightly browned in spots on the outside and tender on the inside, 20 to 25 minutes.

CARAMELIZED ONIONS

ONIONS OFTEN PROVIDE THE MISSING element to many dishes that seem to be lacking something, and even a tablespoon of chopped onion can transform everything from potato salad to pasta sauce. But when do onions really have their moment? Here—caramelized in a heavy pot, left to ooze their own sugars until they create their own sauce. It might just be kitchen alchemy at its finest. All it takes is butter and time.

In the spring or summer, you might find "fresh eating onions." These tend to be attached to their greens and are sometimes small and sold as "babies." They aren't cured for storage, so treat them like any fresh vegetable, storing them in the fridge in plastic and eating them within two weeks. These fresh onions are incredibly juicy, great raw, and ideal for the grill. And caramelized, they're outrageously delicious. That said, you can caramelize any onion—white, yellow, fresh, cured, or anything in between. Just keep in mind that the moisture content will dictate the time it takes to really get those onions caramelized. A regular stored onion might get there in 25 minutes, but a juicy, fresh eating onion will take upward of 60 minutes.

This recipe makes a lot, because if I'm going to put all that time into slicing and cooking, I want to have a solid container of onions to show for it. They're good in the fridge for about 5 days, and I recommend freezing them in ½-cup portions. They defrost as good as new, and then you have a shortcut for Caramelized Onion Dip (page 246) or Pissaladière (page 244).

MAKES 2 TO 2½ CUPS

2 tablespoons unsalted butter
2 tablespoons olive oil
3 pounds onions, halved and thinly sliced
½ teaspoon kosher salt

1. Heat the butter and the oil in a large, heavy-bottomed pot or Dutch oven over medium heat. When the butter melts, stir in the onions and salt. Cover the pot and cook, setting your timer to stir every 10 minutes, until the onions turn gold and the bottom of the pan is coated with a brown crust. (If the onions begin to burn at any point, reduce the heat to medium-low.) This will take anywhere from 30 to 60 minutes, depending on the moisture content of the onions.

2. When the onions are ready, use a wooden spoon or spatula to scrape the brown bits from the bottom of the pan, stirring to integrate the bits into the onions. Keep the pot uncovered, cooking and scraping until the onions are a deep golden brown, another 2 to 3 minutes.

SIMPLE SWEET POTATOES

THIS REALLY IS BARELY A RECIPE, YET somehow this is one that I've written down over and over for people. Although the sweet potatoes cook in the oven, they're really steamed, because the dish gets covered in aluminum foil to trap the moisture. Most vegetables have a nice gradation of doneness, and you can choose your endpoint based on your preference. Some like broccoli raw, others like it grassy and just barely cooked, and then some people like it cooked forever. Sweet potatoes are different—they are undercooked until they're cooked. Bite into a sweet potato when it's not quite ready and it tastes like a half-cooked carrot. But in that moment when they go from uncooked to cooked, the flesh turns incredibly sweet and creamy. Your fork should go right through it without any give, and in the case of a garnet sweet potato (my favorite variety), the flesh will turn a bright autumn-leaf orange. Don't try to eat it before it hits that magic moment.

Sweet potatoes are not actually related to potatoes but are the edible star of the morning glory family. They are also not yams, although they're often mislabeled as such. Actual yams—which are much drier and starchier—grow primarily in Africa and Asia, and they don't tend to make it into our Western markets. Most of the sweet potato varieties you'll find cook up soft and creamy, but you might occasionally come across drier varieties in Asian and Latin markets.

SERVES 4

2½ pounds sweet potatoes (3 to 4), cut into 1½-inch-thick rounds
1 tablespoon olive oil
½ teaspoon kosher salt

1. Preheat the oven to 400°F.

2. Pack the sweet potato rounds into a 9 × 13-inch or similar baking dish. Top with an even drizzle of the olive oil and sprinkle of the salt. Tightly cover the dish with aluminum foil.

3. Roast until the sweet potatoes are silky and tender all the way through, 45 to 55 minutes.

MAPLE-BAKED WINTER SQUASH

THE WORLD OF WINTER SQUASH IS WIDE and colorful. Usually only the butternut and acorn varieties make it to the supermarket, but dig through the bins at any October farmers' market or farm stand and you might find everything from the sweet dumpling to the delicata. Each of these squash has a different taste and texture. Some lean toward silky, and others are creamy and starchy. It's worth trying something new, so you can develop a favorite. One squash I always look for is called carnival. It's small and striped, with a squat round shape. It cooks more quickly than an acorn squash, and the skin is tender and great to eat. It doesn't store as well (hence its absence from the grocery store), so when you find one, scoop it up and roast it.

This is a classic way to prepare small winter squash, and the added richness from the maple and butter make it almost dessert-like. You can also add cinnamon and nutmeg to the butter, if you really want to go all the way with the sweetness. If you don't have maple syrup, this is also delicious with brown sugar.

SERVES 4

Neutral oil, such as grapeseed or sunflower, for greasing the baking sheet

2 carnival, delicata, acorn, or other small winter squash

4 tablespoons (½ stick) unsalted butter

3 tablespoons maple syrup

¼ teaspoon kosher salt

1. Preheat the oven to 375°F. Grease a baking sheet with oil.

2. Cut each squash in half through the stem. Scoop out the seeds and compost or roast them (see page 70). Use your knife to make shallow crosshatches in the flesh of each squash half. Put the squash halves, flesh-side down, on the prepared baking sheet and roast for 20 minutes.

3. Remove the baking sheet from the oven and carefully turn over each squash half. Place a tablespoon of butter into the cavity of each squash, and drizzle the maple syrup over all 4 halves. (Each half will get 2 teaspoons of syrup.) Sprinkle with the salt, then return the baking sheet to the oven. Roast until the sauce caramelizes and the squash halves are entirely tender, 25 to 40 minutes, depending on the size and variety. Serve with a spoon so each diner can dig into the sauce that gathers in the heart of each squash half.

BUTTERNUT SQUASH PUREE

BUTTERNUT SQUASH IS THE MOST BORING of the winter squashes, but it's usually inexpensive, easy to find, and it blends into a sweet and creamy puree that lends itself to all sorts of good dishes. I think of butternut squash puree more as an ingredient than a recipe, and when there are big piles of the vegetable on sale at the supermarket or farmers' market, I buy enough to fill my freezer with this puree. Later I can defrost a container to make Butternut Squash Lasagna (page 191) or Butternut Squash Custard with Bourbon Pecans (page 254). If you know you'll be using your puree for savory dishes, use the garlic and sage to infuse the squash as it roasts, but if you want to use it for the custard, keep it more neutral. You can also prepare the butternut squash in the pressure cooker. Seed the squash, cut it into pieces small enough to fit in your cooker, and cook under high pressure with a bit of water for 15 minutes.

This is also a great method for making pumpkin puree. Cut pumpkins in half or quarters, and proceed as below, roasting them at 350°F.

MAKES 8 TO 10 CUPS

Neutral oil, such as grapeseed
7 pounds butternut squash (2 to 3 squash)
Optional: 1 head of garlic, separated into peeled cloves; 10 fresh sage leaves

1. Preheat the oven to 400°F. Grease two large baking dishes or rimmed baking sheets with oil.

2. Cut each squash in half lengthwise by setting it upright on your counter and cutting straight down. Scoop out the seeds with a spoon for composting or set them aside for roasting (see page 70). Lay each half cut-side down on the prepared baking dish, and, if you're using the garlic and sage, lift each squash half up to tuck a few garlic cloves and sage leaves into the cavity.

3. Roast the squash until the skin bubbles and wrinkles and the meat is very soft, 60 to 90 minutes, depending on the size of your squash. Remove them from the oven, turn them over away from you to release the steam, and let the squash cool for at least 30 minutes. Using a small knife or spoon, separate the squash pulp from the skin, and discard the skin and sage, if using. Throw the pulp and the garlic, if using, into a food processor. Working in batches, puree the pulp until smooth. Alternatively, you can mash by hand, adding a bit of water if necessary to help soften the puree. To freeze, transfer the puree to 2-cup freezer-safe containers or bags, and store in the freezer. To use, defrost in the refrigerator.

HOW TO ROAST YOUR SEEDS

Don't throw away those winter squash seeds—they're a bonus ingredient. Scoop out the seeds and the sticky strings around them and place the whole mess in a bowl. Cover the seeds and strings with water and swish it all around with your hands until the seeds rise to the top. Fish out the seeds with your hands or a skimmer. Boil them in salted water for 5 minutes. Drain and dry them as well as you can. Toss the seeds with 1 teaspoon of oil and a pinch of salt per cup of seeds. Add any spices you love—rosemary, curry powder, chili powder, and cumin are all good choices. Roast in a preheated 375°F oven until they pop and sizzle, 15 to 17 minutes, shuffling the seeds halfway through. Eat them as a snack, or add to soups, salads, or roasted vegetables.

MAPLE-GLAZED CARROTS AND PARSNIPS

PARSNIPS ELICIT A STRONG RESPONSE. There are parsnip lovers who will order them any time they're on a menu, jumping at the mention of strange concoctions like parsnip spice cake and parsnip ice cream, while others squirm at the sweet and creamy quality of the root vegetable, usually blaming their aversion on the disconcerting starchiness. A few good parsnip dishes usually bring those people around, though.

Parsnips look like white carrots, though thicker at the stem side and more tapered toward the end of each root. I peel both carrots and parsnips, as the peels can hold some bitterness. You can eat parsnips raw, but they shine when cooked, whether combined with other roasted root vegetables, cooked down to a puree, or caramelized and glazed in a pan like in this dish. If you're someone who often relies on potatoes to fill out soups and other dishes, parsnips will take you in a new direction. Think of the flavor as somewhere between a potato and carrot, with all the good qualities of both. I love to combine parsnips and carrots, because they look alike but taste so different. Glazing them in maple syrup and balsamic vinegar really highlights the sweetness of both, and the quick in-the-pan nature of this recipe makes it an ideal weeknight dish. Save any leftovers and top them with a fried egg the next morning.

SERVES 4 TO 6

2 tablespoons unsalted butter

1 pound carrots (about 4 large), peeled, sliced lengthwise, and cut into 1-inch chunks

1 pound parsnips (6 to 7), peeled, sliced lengthwise, and cut into 1-inch chunks

2 tablespoons maple syrup

1 tablespoon balsamic vinegar

1 tablespoon Dijon mustard

¼ teaspoon kosher salt, plus more as needed

Freshly ground black pepper

1. Melt the butter in a 10- to 12-inch skillet set over medium heat. Add the vegetables, cover the skillet, and let the vegetables cook undisturbed until their edges caramelize and turn golden, 7 to 11 minutes. Parsnips have a tendency to burn, so check on the vegetables once or twice, lowering the heat if they begin to burn. Gently stir the vegetables and continue to cook, stirring occasionally, until they are tender, 3 to 5 more minutes.

2. While the vegetables cook, whisk together the maple syrup, vinegar, and mustard in a small bowl.

3. Pour the maple syrup mixture over the tender vegetables and increase the heat to medium-high. Cook, stirring constantly, as the liquid bubbles up and thickens into a glaze, 2 to 3 minutes. Add the salt and lots of freshly ground pepper. Taste and add more of either if necessary.

SMOKY DELICATA CHIPS

DELICATA SQUASH HAS ALWAYS BEEN MY sweetheart of the winter squashes. It's intensely velvety and flavorful, but I also love it for the name, which just *sounds* like something I want to eat. Delicata. Delicata. Delicata.

This oblong and wavy-skinned squash is really more of a fall squash than a winter one. It doesn't store as long as your butternut and acorn because its skin and flesh are more, well, delicate. All winter squash have edible skin, but the delicata's striped skin is especially tender. The flesh is sweet and creamy, and the dips and grooves in the skin create the appearance of a flower when you cut it in a cross section. It's perfect for stuffing, but I love to eat it on its own, roasted into tender bites with a little olive oil and smoked paprika. This recipe works equally well for dinner as a predinner or party snack. We call them chips, but they don't really crunch unless you've got a burnt bit, which is pretty delicious. They're more chips in the sense that you just can't stop eating them.

SERVES 4

3 tablespoons olive oil, plus more for greasing the baking sheet

2 pounds delicata squash (2 to 3 squash), washed, ends cut off, halved lengthwise, seeded, and cut crosswise into ¼-inch slices

1 teaspoon smoked paprika

½ teaspoon kosher salt

Optional: Large flake sea salt, such as Maldon, or smoked salt

1. Preheat the oven to 400°F. Grease a baking sheet with oil.

2. Combine the delicata slices with the 3 tablespoons of olive oil, paprika, and kosher salt. Lay the slices out in a rough single layer on the prepared baking sheet. Roast, shuffling occasionally, until the slices become tender all the way through and deepen in color, 30 to 35 minutes. Remove the tray from the oven and taste a piece. If you prefer to up the saltiness, finish the chips with a sprinkle of sea salt.

GINGER-PICKLED CARROTS

THIS IS A CLASSIC FRIDGE PICKLE—SPICY, sour, and crunchy. They're so good right out of the jar, but these spicy carrots also make zingy additions to potato and grain salads, sandwiches, and really anything that needs a little punch. These pickles will keep in the fridge for months, but when the carrots are gone, just shove more vegetables in there— the brine will work its magic on anything from green beans to radishes to fennel.

MAKES 1 PINT

2 inches fresh ginger, unpeeled, cut into ¼-inch-thick coins

2 garlic cloves

8 ounces carrots (about 2 large), peeled and cut into sticks to fit your jar

1 cup warm water

2 teaspoons kosher salt

1 tablespoon honey

¾ cup apple cider vinegar

¼ teaspoon crushed red pepper flakes

1. Put the ginger and garlic in the bottom of a 2-cup wide-mouth jar. Pack the carrots into the jar vertically.

2. Combine the water, salt, honey, vinegar, and red pepper flakes in a separate jar. Top it with its lid, and shake vigorously to combine. Pour the brine over the carrots until it just covers them. Top the carrot jar with a lid and refrigerate for at least 24 hours before you eat the carrots. Any leftover brine can be stored in the refrigerator for future pickles.

PANFRIED BRUSSELS

FOR YEARS I'VE WORKED AT THE HOLIDAY farmers' markets in my town, so I've come to understand the passion Brussels sprouts can inspire. There are always a limited number of stalks, each thick and woody, far too large to fit in your fridge and too tough to shove in your compost. Each towering stalk has a couple dozen perfect sprouts, round and alive as if the stalk were rooted in some beautiful field. It's a pastoral image for sure, and at the market there's some prestige in having a few honking stalks protruding from your canvas shopping bag. But when supplies get low, I have seen more than one shopper over the years dive for the bin, grab the first stalk they find, and use it to fend off other shoppers while they choose exactly the right stalk.

Brussels sprouts are, not surprisingly, related to cabbage. Although the flavor of Brussels sprouts has some similarity to the sweet nuttiness of cabbage, the texture is really different. The leaves are silky and thin, and the sprouts themselves are excessively tender. For years, the traditional way to cook them was to boil them, and this inevitably overcooked the sprouts and would make the cook's house smell like stinky socks. Luckily, boiling has been replaced by roasting or, my favorite, panfrying. I learned this method from Heidi Swanson in her book *Super Natural Cooking*, and I've never gone back to any other. Although it can feel a little fussy to place each sprout cut-side down on the cast-iron pan, it's really worth it.

SERVES 4

1 pound Brussels sprouts
2 teaspoons olive oil
1 tablespoon neutral oil, such as grapeseed or sunflower
Kosher salt
Freshly ground black pepper
Optional: 2 tablespoons finely grated Parmesan cheese

1. Remove any loose leaves from the sprouts and trim off any stems. Cut each sprout in half through its stem. Put the sprouts into a bowl, add the olive oil, and toss to coat the sprouts in oil.

2. Heat your largest skillet over medium heat. (This is a good time for cast iron if you have it.) Add the neutral oil, rotating the pan to spread the oil. Place the Brussels sprouts in the pan, cut-side down, in as close to a single layer as possible. Sprinkle the sprouts with salt and cover the skillet. If you don't have a lid that fits the pan, a baking sheet will do the job. Let the sprouts sit undisturbed until they begin to color on the cut sides, 4 to 6 minutes. Carefully taste a sprout to see if it's cooked all the way through. If not, replace the cover and cook for a few more minutes.

3. Uncover the skillet and increase the heat to medium-high. Continue to cook, stirring frequently, until the sprouts are golden on all sides, 4 to 6 minutes. Sprinkle with salt, pepper, and cheese, if using.

A POT
OF SOUP

IN CERTAIN MOMENTS, I THINK ABOUT WHICH POT I'LL GIVE TO EACH of my kids when they move into their first kitchen. When I left home, my mother gave me her stainless-steel steamer pot. It was, in essence, two pots in one, since it had a shallow steamer insert. It was impossible to discern the brand or the place where it was made, but it held up well and was the right size for nearly everything I knew how to make. She'd used it through most of her adult life, and then she passed it on to me. And one night when the girls were little and I was stressed and sleep deprived, I got the broccoli steaming and walked away. By the time I remembered, the water was long gone and the pot had buckled and scorched. I knew I was lucky not to have started a fire, but when the pot cooled enough for me to be able to touch it, I held it in both hands and cried. I tried to use it again, but it would pop and groan and jump from the burner whenever it touched the heat.

In my search for a replacement, I learned how rare a good steamer pot really is. I wrestled with steamer baskets and Asian bamboo steamers, and I went through a few pots with poorly fitting glass lids. But I've never found a pot like my mother's steamer.

That pot was actually my only one for my first years on my own, so it boiled pasta and eggs, and it was just the right size for a four-person batch of soup. And when it comes to soup pots, I've known all kinds. There was my very first Le Creuset my friend gave us as a wedding gift: flame orange, a little bit too small, but stunning with its heaviness and immortal white enamel. There was the vintage Copco I bought on eBay for ten bucks, bright red on the outside but scarred on the inside, and with a silly lid that required a pot holder to remove. There was the delicate blue Dansk that my husband found for me at our local dump. And then there's the Le Creuset I finally bought myself when I sold my second book—an epic 9-quart deep marine-blue trough, sized for the way I really make soup.

And which one will go to each of my girls? It's hard to say without knowing who they'll be. Brightly colored cast iron? Sleek and practical stainless steel? Whatever it is, it will be just perfect for a pot of soup.

ROASTED TOMATO AND VEGETABLE SOUP

MAKES JUST UNDER 2 QUARTS

THE METHOD IN THIS RECIPE IS SO SATIS-fying. All the ingredients go onto a baking sheet, and the oven does the work for you. Roasting everything from the tomatoes to the celery gives the soup a deep sweetness, and the carrots make it unexpectedly rich. It's great early fall dinner fare and perfect, of course, with a good grilled cheese. Because roasting brings out the best in even winter supermarket tomatoes, feel free to make this all year round. That being said, this soup also freezes well, so it's a good way to preserve tomatoes right at the end of the season. Just leave out the cream, and add it later when you pull out the soup in January.

2½ pounds tomatoes, cored and cut into large chunks

2 teaspoons fresh oregano leaves

2 stalks celery (with leaves if they look good), cut into 2-inch lengths

1 medium onion, peeled and cut into 8 wedges

4 medium carrots (8 ounces), sliced lengthwise, and cut into 2-inch lengths

Olive oil

Kosher salt

1 head of garlic

½ cup chicken or vegetable stock or water, plus more as needed

½ cup heavy cream

20 fresh basil leaves, plus extra for garnish

1. Preheat the oven to 400°F. Line a rimmed baking sheet with parchment paper.

2. Lay the tomato wedges on the baking sheet and scatter the oregano leaves over them. Arrange the celery, onion, and carrots on the sheet as well. Don't be afraid to pack it, as nothing really needs space. Drizzle olive oil over the vegetables and lightly sprinkle with ¾ teaspoon salt.

3. Peel the outer paper from the head of garlic, and slice the top off the head just enough to expose the cloves. Wrap the head up in aluminum foil like a present, leaving the

(recipe continues)

top open. Pour a glug of olive oil into the top of the bulb, and seal the foil. Add the wrapped garlic to the baking sheet, taking care not to touch any tomatoes with it to prevent them from absorbing the flavor of the foil. Roast until the onions crisp up around the edges, the carrots are soft, and the tomatoes plump up and begin to release their juices, 45 to 50 minutes. Remove the baking sheet from the oven, unwrap the garlic, and let the vegetables cool until you can handle them.

4. Transfer the vegetables and any pan juices to a blender. Squeeze the sweet roasted garlic cloves into the blender as well. Add the stock, cream, basil, and ½ teaspoon salt. (If you have a large high-speed blender you can do this all in one go, but if your blender is smaller, divide the vegetables and liquid into two or three batches.) Add more stock to thin the soup, if you wish. Taste and add salt if necessary. Serve in bowls with a few torn basil leaves, for garnish.

NETTLE SOUP

THE BEST THING ABOUT THE FORAGING craze is that it gives us an excuse to eat our own weeds. Stinging nettles lose their sting as soon as they hit heat. To get them from your yard to the heat, all you need are a pair of rubber or gardening gloves and some scissors. And the reward is worth the risk. Nettles cook down like spinach, but they impart a rich, buttery, almost hazelnut-y quality to any dish they occupy. They're incredibly nutritious, and they answer a distinct craving that hits me just about when nettles show up in the wild.

Think of this soup as spring tonic, ideal for that moment when one more root vegetable just might do you in. It's a rich, green, salty broth, both simple and fancy. I make a pot and heat it one mug at a time, but it's also pretty and delicious enough to serve as an impressive first taste at a dinner party. It's rich enough from just the nettles, but you can gild the lily by swirling a little crème fraîche in the center. And if it isn't nettle season or you just can't find them, spinach is a decent second choice. The flavor will be grassier and less rich but still wonderful. Simply cook the spinach for a minute longer than the nettles in the broth.

SERVES 4 TO 6

6 cups water

1½ cups sliced leeks (about 1 leek, using all the white and tender part of the green)

2 teaspoons roughly chopped peeled fresh ginger (from a 1- to 2-inch piece)

1 bunch watercress, leaves and stems (about 6 ounces), roughly chopped

4 ounces nettles or tender spinach

2 cups chicken or vegetable broth

1 teaspoon kosher salt (omit if your broth is salted)

For serving: Lemon wedges, olive oil, and/or crème fraîche

1. Bring the water to a boil over high heat in a medium saucepan. Add the leeks and cook until they are bright green and barely tender, about 3 minutes. Add the ginger and watercress, and cook for 1 more minute. Then, taking care not to touch them, add the nettles, pushing them down into the water. Cook just until the spikes are tamed, about 10 seconds for early-season nettles and 30 seconds for later-season nettles. Use tongs or a skimmer to transfer the vegetables and ginger to a blender.

2. Place a fine-meshed sieve over a large measuring cup and measure 2 cups of cooking liquid, letting the sieve strain out any grit. Place 1½ cups of the liquid into the blender, reserving the remaining liquid in case the soup needs thinning. Add the broth and salt (if it needs it) to the blender and blend until the soup is very smooth, about 30 seconds in a high-speed blender and 1 to 2 minutes in a regular blender. If you have a smaller blender, do this in two batches.

3. Rinse out the pot, and return it to medium heat. Pour the soup into the pot and heat until steaming. Thin the soup with some of the reserved vegetable cooking water, if necessary, tasting to see if it needs more salt as well. I like this soup to be a bit thick and creamy, but it's also wonderful thinned to the consistency of broth. Remove the pot from the heat and serve in small bowls or cups, with lemon wedges and a drizzle of olive oil or a dollop of crème fraîche, if desired.

HAKUREI
TURNIP SOUP

EARLY ON IN MY FOOD WRITING LIFE, I wrote about a version of this soup, a recipe I'd gotten from Alice Waters. The blog post was called "Sex and the Turnip." (Analytics tells me this post still comes up quite a bit in *certain* Google searches.) I felt then, as I do now, that the Hakurei turnip belongs in the ranks of oysters and chocolate—that its curvy smooth flesh qualifies it for aphrodisiac status. Bite into a raw Hakurei turnip and it gives under your teeth, not with a crunch but with a glide. Cooked, the texture becomes silky and transparent, the taste both sweet and bitter at once. It's best raw, caramelized (see page 27), or like this, in a simple soup that gives the sexy turnip a bath in which to lounge.

This recipe is quite close to the Alice Waters original, but I couldn't create a collection of simple vegetable recipes without it. It would seem that a soup of just turnips wouldn't be a stunner, but over the years it's never failed to be a showstopper. Try to use really delicious stock here, as the taste will make a big difference. And don't skip the Parmesan—it's essential.

MAKES JUST UNDER 2 QUARTS

1 tablespoon olive oil

1 tablespoon unsalted butter

2 cups thinly sliced leeks (1 to 2 leeks, using all the white and the tender part of the green)

1 tablespoon fresh thyme leaves

Kosher salt

2 bunches Hakurei turnips (about 1¾ pounds), greens separated, turnips quartered and thinly sliced

6 cups chicken or vegetable stock

For serving: Grated Parmesan cheese

1. Heat the olive oil and butter in a large pot set over medium heat. Add the leeks, thyme, and 1 teaspoon salt. Cook, stirring occasionally, until the leeks soften, about 5 minutes. Add the turnips and continue to cook, stirring occasionally, until they are soft and slightly translucent, 4 to 5 minutes.

2. Meanwhile, sort through the turnip greens and discard any withered ones. Rinse the good greens, roughly chop them, and measure out 4 cups. Save any extra for Miso Greens (page 40) or Polenta with all the Greens (page 166).

3. Add the stock to the pot, increase the heat to medium-high, and bring to a low boil. Add the greens to the pot and reduce the heat to medium-low. Cover the pot and cook until the turnips are silky and the greens are tender, 10 minutes. Taste, and add additional salt, as necessary. Serve with lots of Parmesan cheese.

PEA SOUP

THE FIRST NIGHT THIS RECIPE MADE ITS way into the world, I brought it along on a picnic with my friend Emily. I had filled little jars with the precious bright green soup and transported it in a cooler to keep it cold.

"Pea soup!" Emily's eyes got a little far away. "When I was little, my mother used to make pea soup once a year. She'd harvest all the shelling peas at once and all those pods would turn into hardly any peas at all. But she'd blend them into a soup that we'd eat out of teacups. It was so sweet and creamy and green, and we'd lick every bit out of the cup. Once it was gone, it was gone until the next year. There was never a bit left over."

I've eaten Emily's mother's cooking, and I worried that my soup might not live up to her memory. But I handed her a jar and spoon, and I waited.

"And this"—she closed her eyes—"is what it tasted like."

This is a once-a-year soup, a soup to celebrate the very fact of the pea itself. Pick as many peas as you can, and don't worry when they all reduce down to a single cup. That cup is enough, and the resulting soup will be good enough to last in your memory until next year.

MAKES ABOUT 1 QUART

1 tablespoon unsalted butter
½ cup chopped onion (about ½ medium onion)
Kosher salt
1 cup fresh peas (from about 1 pound shelling or English peas)
15 fresh mint leaves
1 cup chicken or vegetable stock
½ cup buttermilk
¼ cup heavy cream
For serving: Crème fraîche, freshly ground black pepper

1. Melt the butter in a small saucepan set over medium heat. Add the onion and cook, stirring often, until soft and translucent, 5 to 7 minutes. Remove the pan from the heat.

2. Meanwhile, bring a small pot of salted water to a boil. Have ready a bowl of ice water nearby. Submerge the peas in the boiling water and cook until bright green, about 30 seconds. Use a slotted spoon to transfer the peas to the ice water and let them cool completely. Drain the peas in a colander.

3. Combine the onions, peas, mint, stock, buttermilk, cream, and 1 teaspoon salt in a blender. Blend until completely smooth, about 30 seconds in a high-speed blender and 90 seconds in a regular blender. Refrigerate for at least 1 hour, then serve in small bowls with a dollop of crème fraîche and a grind of pepper.

CHICKEN SOUP WITH LOTS OF GREENS

LIKE MANY HOME COOKS, MY CHICKEN soup method is from my mother. She's always made soup from the whole chicken, boiling it first to make stock and cook the chicken at the same time. It creates a rich broth, and the mix of white and dark meat makes a tastier soup than one made with only one part of the chicken. Lemon and ginger are also essential to her soup—she just adds huge slices of ginger to infuse the broth. The ginger is meant to be left in the pot, but usually someone gets a chunk and confuses it with a potato, and they get a bonus cleaning out of the sinuses.

The lemon-ginger combination is the foundation with which I create endless chicken soup variations throughout the year, and I like it most when I can pump it up with all the greens in my refrigerator. This soup is so green, so tart and hot—it's the answer to colds, to nights that need extra comfort, or to any craving for a really good chicken soup. Preserved lemon is so perfect, because it takes care of the lemon and the salt in one go. But if you don't have a jar already made in your fridge (see page 57 to make your own), use extra lemon juice and salt right at the end, tasting as you go until it's just right. I love the Asian greens here, but if you have other greens in your fridge or garden, go ahead and use those. It's meant to be a soup of the moment.

MAKES ABOUT 3 QUARTS

1 3- to 4-pound chicken

4 scallions

1 lemon, halved

2 to 3 inches unpeeled fresh ginger, sliced ¼ inch thick

2 cups peeled, quartered, and ½-inch sliced carrots (about 2 large carrots)

2 cups halved, thinly sliced, and washed leeks (1 to 2 leeks, using all the white and the tender part of the green)

Kosher salt

1 bunch watercress (about 6 ounces), stems and leaves roughly chopped

3 cups roughly chopped bok choy, pak choi, tatsoi, Swiss chard, or kale

1 preserved lemon (page 57), seeded and roughly chopped

Optional: 1 jalapeño, seeded and thinly sliced

1. Put the chicken in a large soup pot and just barely cover it with water. Cut the scallions in half crosswise where they flare from a stalk to separate greens, and add the lower parts, one half of the fresh lemon, and the ginger slices to the pot. (Save the scallion greens for Scallion Crepes, page 216, and reserve the other half of the lemon for finishing.) Set the pot over medium-high heat, cover, and bring to a low boil. Uncover the pot, skim off any froth from the surface of the liquid, and reduce the heat to medium-low. Cover the pot again, and cook until the chicken is falling off the bone, about 1 hour. Use tongs or two large spoons to transfer the chicken to a large bowl or platter and let cool until you can handle it. Fish any chicken parts, as well as the scallion roots and the lemon half, out of the pot. You should have a big pot of broth with only the ginger slices floating in it.

2. While the chicken cools, start building the soup. To the pot of broth, add the carrots, leeks, and 1 tablespoon salt. Increase the heat to medium, cover the pot, and cook until the carrots are soft and the leeks are tender, 15 to 20 minutes. Add the greens, preserved lemon, and jalapeño, if using. Cover the pot and cook until the greens are soft and melting into the soup, 5 to 7 minutes.

3. Tear the chicken meat off the bones, shredding it into large pieces as you add it to the soup. Add the juice from the remaining half of the lemon. Taste and add salt, if necessary.

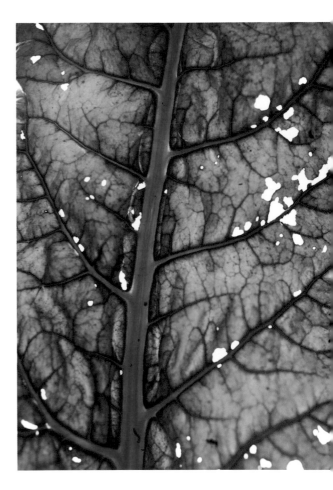

SHIITAKE
BARLEY SOUP

MOST FARMERS' MARKETS HAVE A MUSH-
room vendor, and it's at ours that I've found
the best mushrooms. My favorites are the
tiered oyster mushrooms, which I simply fry
up in butter, and shiitakes, whose meaty saltiness I find so nurturing. This is my take on
classic mushroom barley soup, made better,
I think, by the ginger and miso and a quick
stock made of shiitake stems and leek tops
that comes together as I prep the soup. I love
the taste that the scraps bring to the broth,
and it's nice to use every bit of both the mushrooms and the leeks.

This soup is an ideal recipe if you're not
feeling well, or when looking for a good soup
to bring to a friend who needs extra support.
The creamy barley and salty shiitakes are an
especially comforting combination.

MAKES ABOUT 1½ QUARTS

2 medium leeks

6 ounces fresh shiitake mushrooms

2 to 3 inches fresh ginger

6 cups water

Splash of distilled, wine, or cider vinegar

2 tablespoons olive oil

2 teaspoons tamari or soy sauce

½ cup pearled barley

1 cup roughly chopped spinach
(about 2 ounces)

¼ cup miso paste (red, white, or a
combination)

¼ cup thinly sliced scallions (whites and
light greens)

½ sheet nori seaweed, cut into matchsticks
with scissors

1. First, get the broth together. Cut off the root and toughest part of the green of each of the leeks, tossing the green scraps into a large saucepan. Cut the stem off each shiitake, and toss the stems into the saucepan as well. Peel the ginger with the tip of a spoon, and add the peels to the saucepan. Top off the scraps with the water, cover, and bring the mixture to a boil over high heat. Reduce the heat to medium-low to bring the liquid to a lively simmer. Let the stock cook while you begin the soup.

2. Cut each leek in half lengthwise and slice into thin half-moons. Put the leek slices in a bowl, cover with water, and add the vinegar to help release the grit. Use a damp cloth to wipe the surface of each mushroom. Slice the mushroom caps into ¼-inch slices. Finally, mince the ginger; you should have about 3 tablespoons.

3. Heat the oil in a medium stockpot or saucepan over medium heat. Use a slotted spoon or skimmer to lift the leeks out of the water, shaking them over the bowl to get rid of excess moisture. Add the leek and ginger to the oil and cook, stirring frequently, until the leeks are soft, 3 to 4 minutes. Add the shiitakes and tamari, and continue to cook, stirring occasionally, until the shiitakes shrink, first turning white and then deepening to a very light brown, about 7 minutes. Stir in the barley. Set a fine-meshed strainer over the pot, and pour in the mushroom-leek stock, discarding the scraps. Cover the pot, bring to a boil, and lower the heat to medium-low. Cook, covered, until the barley is tender and the broth is a bit creamy, 18 to 20 minutes.

4. Stir in the spinach and continue to cook for another 2 minutes. Remove the pot from the heat. Measure the miso into a small bowl or measuring cup and use a ladle to add a bit of liquid from the soup to the miso paste. Stir, and keep adding liquid until the miso is the texture of thin pureed soup. Pour the miso into the pot, stirring to combine. Taste the soup, and add a bit more tamari if it needs more seasoning. Ladle into bowls, and top with scallions and nori matchsticks.

CORN CHOWDER

THIS IS STRAIGHT-UP CLASSIC CORN chowder. I only make corn chowder a few times a summer, when I happen to have an excess of corn, a few hands to help shuck it without too much complaining, and enough people to fill the table outside in the yard. It doesn't need much, as the corn really carries it. Save this recipe for the moment when the corn is fresh and sweet—that's when this soup will be its best. Serve it with any simple green or tomato salad and a great loaf of bread, and just let summer do its thing. Make this out of season with frozen corn, or up the spice and add ½ cup diced roasted green chiles along with the corn.

MAKES JUST UNDER 2 QUARTS

4 large ears or 8 small ears of corn
1 bay leaf
1 cup whole milk
2 tablespoons unsalted butter
1½ cups chopped onion (1 to 2 onions)
½ cup chopped celery (1 stalk)
1 cup finely chopped red bell pepper
2 tablespoons fresh thyme leaves
2 teaspoons kosher salt
Freshly ground black pepper
½ cup roughly chopped flat-leaf parsley

1. Use a sharp knife to separate the kernels from each ear of corn, tossing the cobs into a wide pot. In the end, you should have 4 cups of corn. Cover the cobs with water, add the bay leaf, and cover the pot. Bring to a boil over medium-high heat, and then reduce the heat to medium-low. Cook for at least 15 minutes, but it can simmer on the stove for up to 2 hours.

2. Combine 1 cup of the corn with the milk in a blender. Blend until smooth, and set aside.

3. Melt the butter in a heavy-bottomed pot over medium heat. Add the onion and cook, stirring frequently, until softened, 3 to 4 minutes. Add the celery, bell pepper, thyme, and salt, and cook, stirring often, until the bell pepper is tender, 5 to 7 minutes. Add the rest of the corn and 2 cups of hot liquid from the cob pot. Cover and reduce the heat to medium-low. Cook until the corn is tender, 8 to 10 minutes.

4. Add the pureed corn to the soup. Finish with pepper, the parsley, and salt if needed.

ROASTED TOMATILLO AND BLACK BEAN CHILI

IF YOU FIND YOURSELF IN A TOMATILLO patch before the fruit is ready, you'll see a fleet of lime-green paper lanterns, each self-inflated around a tiny green fruit at its top. As the tomatillo grows, it fills the lantern, eventually occupying the full sphere. When a tomatillo is bright green and its walls touch the lantern, it's young but okay to eat. These bright green tomatillos are very tart and crisp, and their skin is sticky. As the tomatillo continues to ripen, the fruit turns pale yellow and bursts out of its lantern, which first dries out and goes brown, then disintegrates into a husk like an abandoned snakeskin. Fully mature tomatillos are often harvested right from the ground, where they fall to tell us they're ready to become salsa. If you're buying tomatillos at the farmers' market or supermarket, you'll often find them at this point—pale greenish yellow with a few bits of husk still clinging to them.

And mostly, salsa is what they do become. Tomatillos are a staple in many Central and South American cuisines, and while they're edible raw, they're often roasted or grilled before being blended into salsa verde.

I find that roasted tomatillos have a particular affinity for black beans, and that's how this chili came about. It is a fairly spicy chili and makes use of single-chile powder, which is different from mixed chili powder. But if your spice meter is lower, reduce or omit the chile powder.

SERVES 8

2 pounds tomatillos (15 to 20), separated from their husks and quartered

Kosher salt

2 tablespoons neutral oil, such as grapeseed or sunflower, plus more as needed

1 pound ground turkey, chicken, or beef

2 cups chopped onions (1 to 2 onions)

1 cup chopped celery (from about 2 stalks)

1 to 2 jalapeño peppers (or other hot peppers), seeded and finely chopped

1 tablespoon dried chipotle chile powder

1 teaspoon ground cumin

2 teaspoons dried oregano

1 tablespoon finely minced garlic (3 to 5 cloves)

6 cups cooked black beans in their liquid (from about 1 pound of dried black beans) or 3 15-ounce cans beans, drained

For serving: Grated Cheddar or Monterey Jack cheese, hot sauce, sour cream or crème fraîche, lime wedges, diced avocado

(recipe continues)

1. Preheat the oven to 450°F. Line a rimmed baking sheet with parchment paper, and arrange the tomatillos on the baking sheet. Sprinkle the tomatillos with salt and roast until they collapse and begin to color, 25 to 30 minutes. Set aside.

2. Meanwhile, heat the 2 tablespoons of oil over medium-high heat in a large, heavy-bottomed pot. Add the ground meat and cook, stirring often, until it releases liquid, reabsorbs it, and begins to brown, about 10 minutes. Add a bit more oil if the pan dries out. Lower the heat to medium-low and add the onions, celery, jalapeños, chile powder, cumin, oregano, and 1 tablespoon salt. Cook, stirring often, until the whole mixture softens and shrinks, about 15 minutes. Add the garlic and cook, stirring often, for another 5 minutes.

3. Add the tomatillos and any liquid that has gathered on the baking sheet. Stir in the beans, and bring the mixture to a low boil. Cover the pot, reduce the heat to medium-low to maintain a low simmer, and cook, stirring occasionally, until the ingredients have melded together, about 30 minutes. Add a bit of black bean liquid or water if the chili gets too thick. Continue to add bean liquid to achieve the texture you prefer. Taste and add salt if needed. Serve with copious toppings on the side.

CARAMELIZED CABBAGE SOUP

IF YOU HAPPEN TO HAVE A COPY OF *THE Homemade Kitchen*, you'll see a photo of me in my spring garden. It looks just as it should: dark, compost-rich beds holding hundreds of little seedlings. It looks like I've planned well and planted a garden that will feed my family through the season.

At least, that's how it *looks*. This is what was really going on in that picture: Under deadline, crazed, and three days away from the first day of photos, I asked my friend Elizabeth over at Indian Line Farm for help. I knew we were taking a garden shot, and at that point, all that was growing in my neglected garden was thistle and last year's rotten kale. She pulled out a few flats of seedlings that had been forgotten and were a bit droopy. She told me they'd perk up enough in the ground to at least look good in my photo. "I'm pretty sure these are all cabbage," she told me. I was so grateful—I didn't care what they were. I figured we'd get the shot, pull out the seedlings, and then I'd start again with the real garden I was planning for the year. Of course, that never happened, and that's how we've come to know that time as the year of the cabbage.

This recipe was one of my favorite new cabbage discoveries, and it is a great way to make use of a lot of cabbage at once. I caramelize the cabbage as if it were onions, add a rich broth, and top it with cheesy toasts. It's sweeter and heartier than onion soup, and it's even turned a few people who thought they didn't like cabbage into big cabbage enthusiasts.

MAKES 2½ QUARTS

SOUP
4 tablespoons (½ stick) unsalted butter

10 cups finely sliced green cabbage (1 large head)

1 medium onion, thinly sliced

2 teaspoons dried thyme

2 quarts chicken or beef stock

1 tablespoon tamari or soy sauce

Kosher salt and freshly ground black pepper

TOASTS
½ stale baguette, cut into ¼-inch slices

½ cup grated Parmesan or Gruyère cheese

1. Make the soup: Melt the butter over medium heat in a large pot or Dutch oven. Add the cabbage and onion and cook, stirring often, until the cabbage wilts, about 10 minutes. Reduce the heat to medium-low, cover the pot, and cook, stirring occasionally, until the cabbage is golden and shrinks by at least half, 35 to 45 minutes.

2. Add the thyme and cook for a few more minutes. Pour the stock into the pot, increase the heat to medium-high, bring to a low boil, and use a wooden spoon or spatula to scrape the brown bits off the bottom of the pot and incorporate them into the broth. Reduce the heat to medium-low, and cover the pot. Cook for 10 minutes. Add the tamari and season with salt and pepper.

3. While the soup cooks, **make the toasts:** Preheat the broiler to 450°F or medium-high, depending on your broiler options. Arrange the bread slices on a baking sheet. Sprinkle generously with the cheese. Keeping a close eye on the toasts, broil until the cheese melts, 1 to 2 minutes.

4. Serve the soup in big bowls, with a few toasts floating in each one.

WINTER BORSCHT

I HAVE ALWAYS BEEN A SUMMER BORSCHT person. Cold, bright pink, herby, and full of buttermilk—I could eat that soup every day. But this simple hot borscht brought me to the other side, and now I embrace both seasons of borscht. I imagined this soup as much more complicated—I wrote recipes that included everything from cabbage to tomato to caraway. But my friend Hedley steered me on the right course, describing a bowl of soup she'd had years ago when she needed it most. She'd never forgotten it: "Just beets and carrots, all boiled in the simplest broth. Then there was lemon, and crème fraîche, and so much parsley right at the end, as if parsley was a leafy green."

I would have never had the courage to simplify it so much, but I made the soup just as she'd described it. There's not even a sauté here—everything just boils, and the result is so good. The vegetables go tender and sweet, bathing in a deep red broth that is simply beet elixir. Crème fraîche or sour cream adds richness, and if you want them, the hard-boiled eggs make it even more of a meal. But one addition I insist upon no matter what is buttered rye toast. It's essential.

MAKES ABOUT 2 QUARTS

1½ pounds beets (3 to 5 medium beets), peeled and cut into ¾-inch chunks

½ pound carrots (2 large carrots), halved lengthwise, and cut into ¾-inch pieces

2 cups halved and sliced leeks (from 1 to 2 leeks, using the white and tender green parts)

5 cups chicken or vegetable stock

1 bay leaf

Kosher salt

Freshly ground black pepper

1 lemon, cut in half

For serving: Crème fraîche or sour cream; 2 cups roughly chopped flat-leaf parsley (about 1 bunch); hard-boiled eggs (optional), sliced; buttered rye toasts

1. Combine the beets, carrots, leeks, stock, and the bay leaf in a large pot set over medium-high heat. Cover the pot, bring the mixture to a low boil, and reduce the heat to medium-low to keep it at a lively simmer. Cook, covered, until the vegetables are quite tender when pierced with a fork, 30 to 35 minutes. Taste the broth. If there's no salt in your stock, add 1½ teaspoons salt. If it's salted at all, add ¼ teaspoon, taste, and add more until it tastes good to you. Remove the pot from the heat, and add lots of fresh pepper. Remove the bay leaf.

2. Ladle the soup into bowls. Give each bowl a generous squeeze of lemon, a scoop of crème fraîche, and a handful of parsley. Serve with sliced hard-boiled eggs, if desired, and buttered rye toasts on the side.

POSOLE

RIGHT AROUND AUGUST 1, I START TO smell roasted green chiles. It's a phantom smell, stuck in my own internal calendar from the years we lived in New Mexico.

Most New Mexican green chiles are grown around the town of Hatch, although farmers in other regions of the state will often grow the fleshy chile as well. In late July, round roasters pop up on the side of the road, spinning the chiles so they roast evenly. The aroma that comes from this process is heady and smoky and sweet all at once.

If green chiles ripen, they become red chiles, and these are dried and ground into a smooth sauce. Every New Mexican dish comes with "green or red," and most people either have a strong preference, or they go for "Christmas," the red smoky, the green acidic.

Sometimes we think about moving back to New Mexico, and the access to chile is one of the first reasons on our list. Instead, we order a box of chiles every August and roast them ourselves on the grill for a year's worth in the chest freezer. The shipping costs are high, but it's cheaper than moving.

Our first chile meal is always posole, a stew of green chile and hominy, a kind of treated corn. You can buy hominy dried and cook it like a grain, but this is one of the few situations when I think the canned version is tastier. Green chiles can vary in heat, so it's good to taste as you go and bring it right to your preference. And if you have leftover pork, chicken, or beef, you can add it for a meaty version. You can also buy canned green chiles, a poor but often necessary substitute. They never seem to be spicy enough, so I always augment canned green chiles with hot sauce.

MAKES ABOUT 2 QUARTS

1 tablespoon olive oil

1 cup minced onion (about 1 onion)

1 tablespoon finely minced garlic

1 tablespoon fresh oregano leaves or 1 teaspoon dried

1 teaspoon kosher salt

2 cups roughly chopped green cabbage

1 pound Yukon Gold potatoes (2 to 3 potatoes), cut into 1-inch chunks

2 15-ounce cans hominy, drained

2½ cups chicken or vegetable stock

1 cup chopped roasted green chiles (from 5 to 7 chiles) or 3 2.75-ounce cans

Optional: 2 cups leftover shredded or cubed chicken, pork, or beef

½ cup roughly chopped fresh flat-leaf parsley or cilantro

For serving: Cubed avocado, crème fraîche or sour cream, lime wedges, hot sauce

1. Heat the olive oil in a heavy pot over medium heat. Add the onion and cook, stirring often, until soft, about 5 minutes. Add the garlic, oregano, salt, cabbage, potatoes, hominy, stock, and ¾ cup of the green chiles to the pot, stirring to combine. Increase the heat to medium-high to bring the mixture up to a boil. Cover, reduce the heat to medium-low, and cook until the cabbage and potatoes are tender, 20 to 25 minutes.

2. Stir in the meat, if using, and parsley. Taste, and add the remaining chiles, if the soup can stand to get spicier. Cook for an additional minute. Serve in bowls with cubed avocado and crème fraîche, with lime wedges for squeezing on the side, and hot sauce, if desired.

CELERIAC AND APPLE SOUP

CELERIAC, ALSO CALLED CELERY ROOT, IS knobby and hairy and can be hard to understand. It's not actually the root of celery, but it's related enough that the flavors of the two vegetables are very connected. It's good raw in a salad (see page 202), roasted with other vegetables, or pureed alone or with potatoes. It's an essential ingredient in my beef stew, as it provides the starch of a potato and the flavor of celery all at once. Blended into a soup, it turns into aromatic silk, hard to identify but very easy to love. It can also tend toward the bitter, so I love to combine it with something sweet.

We have a few apple trees that we adore but don't quite take care of, and I always end up with bushels of deformed and bruised apples. Most become sauce or pie, but I'm often looking for savory ways to use them. That's how this soup was born. Big thanks to Franck Tessier of Chez Nous Bistro in Lee, Massachusetts, for making this recipe truly wonderful. We were both at a country fair, and when he asked me how I was doing, I admitted I had spent the weekend struggling to take this particular recipe beyond just a good soup. He answered, without a pause, "Hazelnuts and Stilton." Of course he was right, and this soup has been in my rotation ever since. If hazelnuts are too pricey or hard to find, pecans are a good second choice.

MAKES 2 QUARTS

2 tablespoons unsalted butter

2 tablespoons olive oil

2 cups sliced leeks (1 to 2 leeks, using all the white and the tender green)

1 cup roughly chopped onion (1 small onion)

1¼ teaspoons kosher salt

¼ teaspoon freshly grated nutmeg

2 teaspoons minced garlic (2 cloves)

1½ pounds celeriac (1 to 2 roots), peeled (see note) and cubed

3 medium apples, peeled, cored, and quartered

4 cups chicken or vegetable stock

1 cup whole milk

Freshly ground black pepper

For serving: 1 cup toasted, roughly chopped peeled hazelnuts; 4 ounces crumbled Stilton or blue cheese

1. Heat the butter and olive oil together over medium heat in a large pot. Let the butter brown just slightly. Add the leeks and onion, and cook, stirring often, until soft and shiny, about 5 minutes. Add the salt, nutmeg, and garlic, and cook for another minute. Add the celeriac, apples, and stock to the pot. Cover, raise the heat to high, and bring the liquid to a boil. Reduce the heat to medium-low and cook, stirring occasionally, until the apples and celeriac fall apart, 20 to 25 minutes.

2. If you have an immersion blender, use it to blend the soup until smooth. Otherwise, transfer the mixture to an upright blender in batches, blend, and return it to the pot. Add the milk, and season with salt and pepper; stir. Scoop into bowls and top each with a handful of nuts and a healthy crumble of cheese.

HOW TO PREPARE CELERIAC

A vegetable peeler is hardly a match for celeriac's rough peaks and valleys. Here's a better way to peel it: First, cut off the knobbiest end. Then slice the rest of the root into 1- to 2-inch rounds. From there, simply use your knife to trim off the edges. If there are deep grooves of the rough peel within the root, dig them out with your paring knife. Once you have peeled rounds, cut or grate them as the recipe requires. Save all your peels in the freezer—they make fantastic additions to stock.

KALE AND WHITE BEAN SOUP WITH ROSEMARY OIL

THERE IS A BAKERY IN SANTA FE, NEW Mexico, called Sage Bakehouse that I used to go to when I was in school. It was all concrete—cavernous and always warm from the ovens. The primary draw was their bread, and they made generous round loaves of sourdough with a soft crust that sliced well. I'd go there to study and order a toast basket: three kinds of toast with a ramekin of strawberry jam. For lunch, there were always great soups. One day when I was there, alone before an afternoon class, I had the white bean soup with garlic and rosemary. I finished my bowl, mopped up the creamy white broth with my bread, walked to the counter, and pleaded for the recipe. The lovely woman with her hair tied back in a kerchief didn't even pause. She recited this recipe from memory.

This became the first soup that took me beyond my mother's soup repertoire. It was a soup that I made for dinner, and then people asked me for the recipe. It also was the recipe that made me feel like I might be able to cook. Over the years there have been endless variations. There could be half a can of crushed tomatoes or a few garlic sausages, cut into little slices. And instead of rosemary, there could always be fresh chopped sage. That being said, the basic recipe is good enough to stick with. I'll leave it to you, and you can do with it what you wish.

MAKES 3 QUARTS

1 pound dried cannellini or navy beans, picked over for stones, soaked in water for 6 to 8 hours, drained

7 peeled garlic cloves

2-inch piece of Parmesan rind, roughly chopped

5 4- to 6-inch sprigs fresh rosemary

1 bay leaf

8 cups chicken or vegetable stock

2 cups water, plus more as needed

1 bunch curly kale (about 8 ounces), stems removed, leaves chopped into fine ribbons

1½ teaspoons kosher salt, plus more as needed

Freshly ground black pepper

¼ cup olive oil

For serving: Grated lemon zest

1. Put the beans in a large, heavy-bottomed pot along with the garlic, Parmesan rind, 3 of the rosemary sprigs, and the bay leaf. Add the stock and water. Cover, set the pot over medium-high heat, and bring to a boil. Reduce the heat to medium-low and cook, stirring occasionally, until the beans are tender, 2 to 2½ hours.

2. Remove the bay leaf and rosemary stems. (The rosemary leaves will be in the soup— that's okay.) Mash some of the beans and garlic with a potato masher or large wooden spoon. Add the kale and salt. If the soup is

(recipe continues)

too thick, add up to 1 cup of water. Increase the heat to medium-high, bring the soup to a low boil, and cover the pot. Reduce the heat to low, and cook, stirring occasionally, until the kale is tender and melts into the soup, 25 to 30 minutes. Taste and add more salt, if needed, and lots of pepper to taste.

3. Meanwhile, heat the oil in a small skillet set over medium heat. Add the remaining 2 rosemary sprigs to the oil, pressing to submerge them. After a moment, the rosemary will sizzle and the smell of rosemary will fill your kitchen. Remove the skillet from the heat and let it sit for 20 minutes to infuse the oil.

4. Serve in large soup bowls, with a drizzle of rosemary olive oil and a grating of lemon zest over each bowl.

BUTTERNUT RED LENTIL DAL

CREAMY DAL IS ONE OF MY GO-TOS, AND like any soup that I've made throughout the years, it tends to change with my tastes and the contents of my refrigerator. I love this version, bright orange and spicy with the combination of butternut squash, carrots, and lots of fresh ginger. The red lentils cook quickly, and if I have butternut squash puree ready to go and defrosted from the freezer, this comes together fast enough for a weeknight dinner.

MAKES 2 QUARTS

2 tablespoons unsalted butter

2 cups chopped onion (1 to 2 onions)

2 teaspoons minced garlic (2 to 3 cloves)

1 tablespoon grated unpeeled fresh ginger (about 3 inches)

¼ teaspoon ground cumin

½ teaspoon ground coriander

⅛ teaspoon cayenne, plus more as needed

½ teaspoon ground nutmeg

2½ teaspoons kosher salt

¾ pound small red or Yukon Gold potatoes (2 to 3 potatoes), peeled and cut into ½-inch chunks

1 cup chopped carrots (1 to 2 carrots)

1 cup rinsed red lentils

5 cups water

2 cups Butternut Squash Puree (page 69)

1. Melt the butter in a large, heavy-bottomed pot set over medium heat. Add the onion and cook, stirring often, until soft and translucent, about 10 minutes. Stir in the garlic, ginger, cumin, coriander, cayenne, nutmeg, and salt.

2. Add the potatoes, carrots, lentils, and water to the pot. Stir, cover, increase the heat to medium-high, and bring the mixture to a boil, stirring occasionally. Reduce the heat to medium-low, and bring the soup down to a simmer. Cover the pot and cook, stirring occasionally, until the potatoes are soft and the lentils begin to break down, about 20 minutes. Stir in the squash puree and cook for another 10 minutes. Taste and add more salt and cayenne, if necessary.

CAULIFLOWER CHEDDAR SOUP

THIS RECIPE IS A GIFT FROM MY FRIEND Marisa McClellan. Her blog *Food in Jars* and book of the same name have helped endless people get over their fear of home canning, and her subsequent books have built on that work, teaching people about small-batch and natural-sweetener preservation. Marisa and I met right around the release of our first books, and since then, we try to get together when we can, usually stealing some time out of a book tour to cook and eat simple comfort food, which is what we usually need just then. This is one of Marisa's favorite soups, and she offered it to me when she took a peek at my recipe list and found it sadly absent of a cauliflower soup. It's really a soup version of Cauliflower Cheese (page 203), creamy and incredibly comforting. I love the method of stirring the cheese sauce into the soup, as it helps to maintain the silkiness of the pureed cauliflower.

MAKES 2½ QUARTS

3½ tablespoons unsalted butter

1 large head of cauliflower (2 pounds), roughly chopped (including the stem)

½ cup chopped carrot (about 1 carrot)

2 cups sliced leeks (1 to 2 leeks, using all the white and the tender green parts)

½ cup dry white wine

4 cups chicken or vegetable stock, plus more as needed

1½ tablespoons all-purpose flour

1½ cups whole milk

1 cup grated Cheddar cheese

4 ounces cream cheese

¼ teaspoon grated fresh nutmeg

Freshly ground black pepper

1 tablespoon kosher salt, plus more as needed

1. Melt 2 tablespoons of the butter in a large pot set over medium heat. Add the cauliflower, carrot, and leeks, and cook, stirring often, until the vegetables soften and begin to color, 8 to 10 minutes. Add the wine and raise the heat to medium-high. As the wine boils, use a wooden spoon or spatula to scrape any brown bits from the bottom of the pot. Add the stock, bring the mixture to a simmer, and cover the pot. Reduce the heat to medium-low, and cook until the vegetables are tender, 10 to 12 minutes.

2. Meanwhile, melt the remaining 1½ tablespoons of butter in a medium saucepan set over medium heat. Whisk in the flour and continue to cook, whisking often, until the mixture becomes golden and smells nutty, 2 to 3 minutes. Add the milk a bit at a time, whisking well after each addition. Cook and stir until the sauce comes to a low boil and thickens, 2 to 3 minutes. Remove the pot from the heat. Add the Cheddar and stir until it melts. Stir in the cream cheese until it fully incorporates into the cheese sauce. Add the nutmeg, several grinds of pepper, and salt.

3. When the vegetables are tender, use an immersion blender to puree the mixture. Alternately you can use a regular blender, working in batches and taking care not to splatter the hot liquid. Either way, the soup will be thick and porridge-like, but feel free to add a bit more stock if you'd like it to be thinner. Stir the thick cheese sauce into the soup. Taste and adjust for salt, if necessary.

CARROT GINGER SOUP WITH CURRY LEAVES

I'VE ALWAYS FOUND CARROT SOUPS TO BE rather unsexy. I think my experiences had involved slightly chunky, thick, and earthy soups that I just wished were made of butternut squash instead. Those bad soups motivated me to create this, one of the sexiest soups I know. Peeled and roasted, carrots blend to a smooth puree, and all that ginger and lime heats and cools at the same time in the most wonderful way.

A few notes on the preparation of this one: There is *a lot* of ginger in this soup, and you want every bit of it. That being said, grating all that ginger is a bit of a chore. It's easier if you have a small ceramic grater (see page 21) and work with a large chunk at once so you have a good handle. Just be patient. Also, this soup is garnished with curry leaves in coconut oil. Curry leaves are not related to curry powder, but they do grow on the curry tree and are used in Indian cooking. They have a unique and wonderful flavor, and there's really no substitute. Buy them fresh at an Indian grocer or in a supermarket with a good produce department, and simply put the leftover fresh leaves right into the freezer in a freezer bag. When you're set to use them, just put the leaves you need on the counter for a few minutes to soften, then they're ready. If you can't find them, just use plain coconut oil.

MAKES ABOUT 2 QUARTS

1 medium onion (8 ounces), cut into wedges

2 pounds carrots (about 8 large carrots), peeled and cut into 1-inch-thick rounds

1 tablespoon neutral oil, such as grapeseed or safflower

1 teaspoon kosher salt, plus more as needed

15 curry leaves

1 tablespoon coconut oil

3 cups vegetable or chicken stock

1 13.6-ounce can coconut milk

3 tablespoons grated unpeeled fresh ginger (about 5 inches)

1 tablespoon fresh lime juice (1 lime)

1. Preheat the oven to 425°F. Line a baking sheet with parchment paper.

2. Toss the onion, carrots, oil, and salt together in a large bowl. Spread on the prepared baking sheet and roast until the carrots are tender and the onion is golden, about 20 minutes.

3. Meanwhile, prepare the curry coconut oil. Roll the curry leaves up in a log and grate them into small flakes with a Microplane. You won't get all of the leaf in there—it's okay if there's a nub left. Heat the coconut oil in a small skillet set over medium heat. Remove the pan from the heat and add the curry leaf flakes. Set aside.

4. Combine the roasted carrots and onion, stock, coconut milk, ginger, and lime juice in a blender. Blend until very smooth, about 2 minutes in a regular blender or 45 seconds in a high-speed blender. Taste and add more salt, if necessary. Transfer to a saucepan to reheat on the stove. Ladle into bowls, and use a spoon to drizzle the curry-leaf coconut oil over each bowl, taking care to include some leaf flakes.

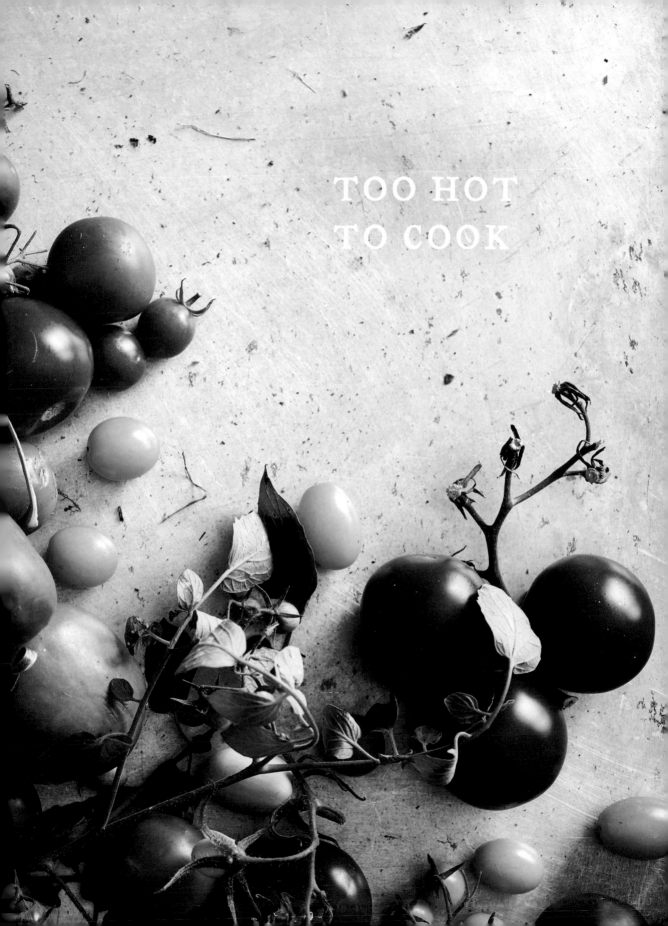

TOO HOT
TO COOK

HOT-WEATHER COOKING IS OFTEN ABOUT FINDING WAYS *NOT* TO COOK. It's a cruel trick to put all the best food within close reach right at the moment when the last thing you want do is turn on the oven. Hard as I try, I can't seem to let a week go by without falling prey to the allure of the oven. So many summer vegetables are so good roasted! If I have roasted beets in the fridge, there are a million things I can make for dinner, starting with Beet and Cucumber Quinoa (page 124), and the list just goes on from there. Pair that with my weakness for pie baking, and you know why you'll find me in a hot, hot kitchen, a fan directed at my face and an ice-cold gin and tonic on the counter. I try to make use of the heat when I've got it and remember that summer is the time to have the fridge well stocked. We cook in the cool early mornings and late nights, packing the oven full of vegetables for all sorts of meals. If the grill is hot, we add enough coals to grill a few extra zucchini or large rounds of fresh onion for another day. Late at night, the coals are the last thing to glow, and it's always nice to have an excuse to sit out and watch the fireflies.

Of course, there are plenty of good summer foods that don't require heat at all. I could be very happy with a full season of Caprese (page 150), Fresh Corn and Stone Fruit (page 145), and Melon with Arugula and Prosciutto (page 160) on rotation for breakfast, lunch, and dinner, with no stove in sight. So we do our best to avoid making more heat, and when we do have to turn on the oven, it better be for something really good.

ZUCCHINI SLAB FRITTATA

MY GRANDPARENTS OWNED A VEGETARIAN bed-and-breakfast, and they cooked through the summer and fall using everything they grew in their 15 × 15-foot backyard garden. I say *their,* but we all know every garden belongs to one side of a couple or the other, and this prolific patch of land fell to the paternal side. My grandfather bravely grew a whole row of zucchini plants, and so several days a week were frittata mornings at the inn. They had more vegetable than egg—really an excuse to blow through several zucchini in one go. I had no taste for it then, but somehow as an adult, long after he was gone, I needed to re-create my grandfather's frittata. Though he grated his zucchini on a box grater and I slice mine fine on a mandoline, I like to think our frittatas have a lot in common. I tend to make this one early in the morning, and then it supplies me with lunch several times during the week; it's so good cold right out of the refrigerator. This is also a great place to use the fresh eating onions you might find at the farmers' market in the summer, as well as any fresh herbs you have in excess.

MAKES ONE 9 × 9- OR 10 × 10-INCH FRITTATA

Neutral oil, such as grapeseed or sunflower

2 pounds zucchini, sliced into paper-thin rounds with a mandoline, food processor, or sharp knife

2 teaspoons kosher salt

1 medium onion (8 ounces), sliced paper thin with a mandoline, food processor, or sharp knife

½ cup mixed fresh herbs, such as basil, rosemary, parsley, or thyme, roughly chopped

½ cup whole-milk ricotta cheese

6 large eggs

4 ounces cream cheese

1¼ cups milk

Freshly ground black pepper

1. Preheat the oven to 350°F. Grease a 9 × 9- or 10 × 10-inch square baking pan with oil.

2. Put the zucchini in a colander and sprinkle with 1 teaspoon of the salt. Gently toss the two together and let sit for 10 minutes to release a bit of liquid.

(recipe continues)

3. Heat 1 tablespoon oil in a large skillet set over medium-high heat. Add the onion and cook, stirring frequently, until soft and translucent, 2 to 3 minutes. Transfer the onion to the prepared baking pan, leaving the skillet on the heat. Add another splash of oil to the skillet. Add half the zucchini to the skillet, giving it a gentle squeeze to remove as much liquid as possible before you put it into the pan. Cook, stirring frequently, until the zucchini slices shrink and start to color, 4 to 5 minutes. Transfer to the baking pan with the onion. Add the second half of the zucchini to the skillet, again giving it a squeeze, adding a bit more oil if the pan seems dry. Add half the herbs and cook, stirring frequently, until the zucchini turns golden, 3 to 4 minutes. Add the herbed zucchini to the baking pan.

4. Combine the ricotta with the remaining herbs and ½ teaspoon salt.

5. Combine the eggs, cream cheese, the remaining ½ teaspoon of salt, the milk, and several grinds of pepper in a blender. Blend until smooth. Pour the custard mixture over the vegetables, then use a tablespoon to dot the top with the herbed ricotta.

6. Bake until the top of the frittata is golden and the center doesn't weep when pricked with a toothpick, 45 to 50 minutes. Allow to cool for at least 20 minutes before serving.

ZUCCHINI AND GARLIC SCAPE PASTA

I EAT ZUCCHINI IN JULY, AUGUST, AND THE first part of September. This is not because I have anything against supermarket zucchini; rather, it's because I don't tend to *choose* zucchini. I eat it when it's free. I eat it when friends are overwhelmed by the fruits of their one-too-many plants in the garden, when kind farmers at the market put a bag of them in my basket as we clean up from the day. I look up and they shrug, admitting they just don't want to bring *all this zucchini* home. So the zucchini find a place in my dinner plan, and usually that is how it happens. And this is the thing: when it's July and it's 90 degrees and I happen to have a half-drunk bottle of wine from the weekend, cold and ready to accompany me as I cook, when the light is coming into the kitchen in that slanty summer way, this is my very favorite thing to cook.

Scapes are the flower of the garlic plant, and the entire stem and flower are edible. They're good grilled, pureed into pasta, or charred in a hot pan, as in this recipe. I love the way the crème fraîche melts into the pasta here, but feel free to use ricotta if that's what you have in the fridge. In many places, garlic scapes hit the markets before zucchini, although here in Massachusetts they come on stage together. But if yours are early, buy extra and store them in the fridge for up to 2 months. They'll be happy to wait for all that zucchini. Or if it's not the moment for garlic scapes, just leave them out entirely. Use any shape of zucchini here—big, little, or round.

SERVES 4

Kosher salt

12 ounces dried linguine, spaghetti, or fettuccine

2 tablespoons olive oil

12 ounces zucchini or other summer squash, quartered and cut into ¾-inch slices

7 to 10 garlic scapes (flowers and stems), roughly chopped

2 tablespoons chopped fresh rosemary

½ cup grated Parmesan cheese

¼ cup crème fraîche

¼ cup thinly sliced fresh basil

Freshly ground black pepper

1. Bring a large pot of salted water to a boil over medium-high heat. Add the pasta and cook until tender, 7 to 10 minutes. Reserve ½ cup of the pasta cooking water, and drain the pasta in a colander.

2. Meanwhile, heat the olive oil in a wide sauté pan or skillet set over medium-high heat. Add the zucchini and ¼ teaspoon salt, and cook for 1 minute. Add the scapes and rosemary, and cook, stirring often, until the zucchini is soft and golden, 4 to 5 minutes. Add ¼ cup of the reserved pasta cooking water. Let the water boil around the zucchini, loosening any brown bits on the bottom of the pan. Continue to cook until the water thickens and gathers around the zucchini in a light sauce, 2 to 3 minutes. Remove the pan from the heat.

3. Transfer the pasta to a wide serving bowl. Sprinkle the cheese over the pasta, then add the zucchini mixture and any sauce in the pan. Add the crème fraîche and a few more spoonfuls of pasta cooking water. Gently toss to thin out the crème fraîche and coat the pasta in the sauce. Top with the basil and lots of black pepper.

BEET AND CUCUMBER QUINOA

IF ALL IS GOING WELL IN MY SUMMER fridge, it contains numerous cold salads I can eat for days. There's a security in seeing them all stacked in their glass containers, like my own personal section of the deli aisle. There's often some version of chickpea salad (like the one on page 135), maybe a potato salad, and always this, my very favorite. I'm not always a quinoa lover, but this is a great place for it— the dressing makes it cold and pickle-y, and it's jeweled with roasted beets and cucumbers that keep crunching up over time. Red quinoa is a bit nuttier than white, and the deep color means the whole thing doesn't turn pink from the beets.

This is also a summer picnic stunner. You can roast the beets Julia-style (see page 36) for this salad; or, if you have a pressure cooker, they go tender in 15 to 25 minutes, depending on their size. Either way, I like to cook up a few bunches of beets at a time so they can be in the fridge and ready to go. If you already have cooked quinoa, this salad comes together quickly, but if you're starting from scratch, give yourself a bit of time to let the quinoa cool.

SERVES 6

1 cup red quinoa

1 ¼ cups boiling water

¼ cup plus 1 teaspoon olive oil

1 ½ teaspoons kosher salt, plus more as needed

8 ounces cucumbers (4 small or 1 big), quartered lengthwise and cut into ½-inch pieces

¼ cup roughly chopped fresh dill

½ cup crumbled or cubed feta cheese

2 scallions (white and light green parts), thinly sliced

3 tablespoons fresh lemon juice (1 lemon)

1 ½ pounds beets (3 to 5 medium beets), cooked, peeled, and cut into small bites

1. Rinse the quinoa in a fine-meshed sieve under cold water. Transfer the quinoa to a medium saucepan set over medium heat, and toast, stirring constantly, until the quinoa dries out and smells nutty, about 2 minutes. Add the boiling water, the 1 teaspoon of olive oil, and ½ teaspoon of the salt, and bring the mixture back to a boil. Cover the pot and reduce the heat to medium-low. Let cook undisturbed for 18 minutes. Remove the pan from the heat, uncover, and fluff the quinoa with a fork. Transfer the quinoa to a bowl about twice as large as you need to hold it. Let cool for a bit at room temperature, then transfer to the refrigerator to cool completely, 30 to 45 minutes.

2. Remove the bowl of quinoa from the refrigerator, gently stirring and tossing the quinoa to fluff it up again. Add the cucumbers, dill, feta, scallions, lemon juice, the remaining ¼ cup of olive oil, and the remaining 1 teaspoon of salt, stirring to combine. Gently fold in the beets. Taste and add more salt, if necessary. The salad will keep in the refrigerator for up to 3 days.

GRILLED BEETS WITH ARUGULA AND CHÈVRE

SUMMER IS THE WORST TIME TO GRILL. I know that grilling keeps the heat outside, that it draws us into the great outdoors, and that it minimizes the dishes. But as my step-father said to me during a grilling lesson, "It's not a good night of grilling unless you're drenched with sweat, you've got ash in your hair, and you get burned at least once."

Still, we grill. We grill meat and vegetables and even fruit. We splurge on flank steak and eat piles of grilled zucchini that drip sweetness and salt. We grill peaches until they create their own caramel, and we grill corn right in its husk and marvel that we'd eat it at any other time, in any other way. But I really head for the grill when the chill comes in at night and we've closed all the windows to keep the afternoon heat in. I want an excuse to stay outside when the days get shorter. Let the rest of the world grill for Fourth of July. The best of grilling season starts on Labor Day.

This is a recipe that will take you from this season into the next. In New England, the fall begins to creep in in early August. It might be a smell or a pocket of cold air in the middle of warmth, but that transition makes it my favorite time of year to cook, inside or out. Of course, the produce is especially good then, and late summer beets are ideal for the grill. They are sweeter and taste more like the earth than beets that have sat in storage, and grilling concentrates the sugar on the crispy edges of each slice. Find nice large beets for this, so you don't lose them through the grates of your grill.

SERVES 4

2 tablespoons olive oil
1 tablespoon plus 1 teaspoon balsamic vinegar
1½ pounds red or golden beets (3 to 5 medium beets), cut into ½-inch slices
4 ounces tender arugula
2 ounces chèvre
Large flake sea salt, such as Maldon
Freshly ground black pepper

1. Heat your grill until it's quite hot.

2. Combine the olive oil with the balsamic vinegar in a small jar, giving it a good shake to emulsify. Paint both sides of each beet slice with the dressing, reserving the leftovers to dress the salad at the end. Grill the beets, taking care not to lose them in the grates of the grill, until tender and brown in spots, 6 to 8 minutes per side. Try a slice and make sure it's tender all the way through. If it's still tough and earthy, give them a few more minutes.

3. While the beets cook, make a bed of arugula on a large platter. Lay the grilled beets out over the arugula, and top with small dollops of chèvre. Drizzle with the remaining dressing. Top with sea salt and freshly ground pepper.

FRISÉE WITH BACON AND AN EGG

FRISÉE, ALSO KNOWN AS CURLY ENDIVE, is a bitter green in the chicory family that's related to radicchio, escarole, and the smaller, dainty Belgian endive. Like its cousins, it has a floral quality that accompanies the bitter, and it can hold up to both cooking and heavy dressing. You'll often find it mixed in with other salad greens—vigorous tumbleweeds of pale green that are beloved by some, hated by others. Because it holds up to heat and dressing, I love it for breakfast with a warm bacon dressing and a poached egg. The egg yolk runs and covers the whole salad. If you don't have or love tarragon, feel free to leave it out, but I find that that the slight licorice sweetness works well with the frisée.

SERVES 4

8 ounces slab bacon or thickly cut bacon, cut into ½-inch pieces
2 tablespoons olive oil, plus more as needed
¼ cup red wine vinegar
1 tablespoon Dijon mustard
1 large head of frisée, separated and torn into bite-sized pieces
Optional: 2 tablespoons roughly chopped fresh tarragon leaves
Kosher salt
4 large eggs
Freshly ground black pepper

1. Heat a medium skillet over medium heat. Fry the bacon in the skillet, stirring often, until crispy, 5 to 7 minutes. Use a slotted spoon to fish out the bacon pieces, transferring them to a bowl. Pour the bacon fat into a large heatproof bowl, then add the olive oil, vinegar, and mustard to the hot bacon fat, whisking well. Add more olive oil if the dressing curdles. Add the frisée, tarragon, if using, and ¼ teaspoon salt to the dressing, tossing gently to coat each leaf in the warm dressing. Divide the greens among four bowls, and sprinkle the bacon bits over each bowl.

2. Bring a small pot of water to a high simmer. (If you start with a wide pan, you can poach 2 eggs at a time.) Crack an egg into a ramekin or teacup and drain off the bit of watery white that will come off first. Make a gentle whirlpool in the water with a spoon, then slide the egg into the water and let it

cook, undisturbed, for about 3 minutes. Use a slotted spoon to transfer the egg to one of the bowls, placing it over the greens. Repeat with the remaining eggs. Sprinkle each bowl, concentrating mostly on the egg, with a bit more salt and lots of freshly ground pepper. Serve immediately.

SWISS CHARD STEM, FENNEL, AND SALMON FRIED RICE

THIS IS ONE OF THOSE DISHES THAT CAME together from bits and scraps, and it was so good we had to give it its own identity. When I cook in the summer, I tend to make extra to cover the days when I don't want to cook, and I'll often have a tub of leftover grains, grilled chicken or fish, and grilled or roasted veggies that make quick work of so many recipes.

The unlikely stars of this fried rice are Swiss chard stems, which I save in a bag in the fridge as I work through the copious summer Swiss chard that tends to come my way. The stems have much more longevity than the leaves; a bag of them can stay fresh for up to 3 weeks. They have a satisfying crunch, a wonderful flavor (think celery meets beet), and if you use stems of rainbow chard, they look like bits of confetti. The salmon can be cooked any way you like here, as you're just going to break it down into bites. If you're planning the week's meals, plan for salmon one day, and use the leftovers the next night.

SERVES 4 TO 6

3 tablespoons neutral oil, such as grapeseed or sunflower

1 cup chopped onion (1 small onion)

12 ounces roughly chopped Swiss chard stems (from about 2 bunches)

1 medium fennel bulb (about 10 ounces), halved and thinly sliced

1 teaspoon kosher salt

3 cups cooked white or brown rice

1 pound cooked salmon, flaked

¼ cup finely chopped fresh dill

For serving: Rice vinegar and tamari or soy sauce

1. Heat the oil in a large skillet set over medium-high heat. Add the onion and cook, stirring frequently, until the onion softens and begins to color, 2 to 3 minutes. Add the Swiss chard stems, fennel, and salt, and continue to cook, stirring often, until both vegetables are tender, about 5 minutes.

2. Fold the rice and salmon into the vegetables, and continue to cook until the salmon is warm and the rice is crispy, 3 to 5 minutes. Transfer to a large platter or wide bowl and top with dill. Serve with the rice vinegar and tamari on the table, so people may season their rice as they wish.

NAPA COLESLAW WITH PECANS AND PEAS

MY AUNT SONDRA, A LONGTIME DEVOTEE of Martha Stewart, taught me how to make this salad when I was a teenager. She'd found some version of it somewhere in the extensive Martha empire and adopted it as her own personal picnic staple. She felt it had the perfect mix of a safe classic and exciting new dish. People would go toward it because it was a classic creamy coleslaw, but the pecans, peas, and tender Napa cabbage would surprise them and cause them to ask for the recipe. Sondra was particularly determined to tame my teenage wildness and school me in the wifely arts of choosing paint colors, ironing, and always knowing the perfect dish to bring to a party. I'm a mess with paint colors, and I don't own an iron, but I think I do pretty well when it comes to party food.

Napa cabbage is also called Chinese cabbage, and it's far more delicate than classic cabbage. It pairs really well with other greens for steaming, and, when dressed and raw, its texture is tender and easy to love. If you have preserved lemons (see page 57) in the refrigerator, feel free to add some chopped rind to this salad; it adds a nice sour punch.

SERVES 6 TO 8

4 heaping cups thinly sliced Napa cabbage (about 1 pound or ½ medium head)

1 cup peas, fresh or frozen (thawed)

1 bunch radishes (5 to 7), chopped

¼ cup thinly sliced scallions (white and light green parts)

½ cup buttermilk

2 tablespoons sour cream, plain yogurt, or crème fraîche

2 tablespoons apple cider vinegar

1 garlic clove, minced or pressed through a garlic press

¼ teaspoon kosher salt

Freshly ground black pepper

1 cup toasted pecans (see page 136), roughly chopped

1. Combine the cabbage, peas, radishes, and scallions in a medium bowl.

2. Stir together the buttermilk, sour cream, vinegar, garlic, salt, and pepper to taste in a small bowl or measuring cup. Pour the mixture over the vegetables, and toss gently to coat the vegetables in the dressing. Top with the pecans.

CREAMY BROCCOLI SALAD

FRESH BROCCOLI THAT YOU GROW OR FIND at a farmers' market or farm stand is far more delicate and sweeter than the heads you'll find at the supermarket all year round. The stems are more tender, and the florets have a nutty flavor that doesn't seem to remain in broccoli that's been out of the ground for a long time. This super-quick cold salad is a good way to celebrate that precious broccoli, as the tarragon helps to bring all those subtle flavors out into the light. This salad can be spicy or mellow, depending on your preference. And it's fantastic (and spicier!) on day two, so it's a good make-ahead for summer picnics and parties. This is also great made with broccolini, the thin bunched cousin of broccoli you might find in the produce aisle.

SERVES 4 TO 6

1 pound broccoli, separated into tall trees
Kosher salt
¼ cup plain yogurt
2 tablespoons mayonnaise
2 teaspoons Dijon mustard
1 tablespoon fresh lemon juice
1 tablespoon roughly chopped fresh tarragon
2 tablespoons finely chopped scallions (white and light green parts)
¼ to ½ teaspoon crushed red pepper flakes

1. Bring a pot of water to a boil. Have ready a bowl of ice water nearby. Add the broccoli and 1 teaspoon salt to the pot, increase the heat to high to bring the water back up to a boil, and cook until just tender, 2 to 4 minutes. Transfer the broccoli to the ice water to cool completely. Drain and dry it on a dish towel. Transfer to the counter, and roughly chop the broccoli. Put it into a serving bowl.

2. Whisk together the yogurt, mayonnaise, mustard, lemon juice, tarragon, scallions, ½ teaspoon salt, and ¼ teaspoon red pepper flakes in a small bowl. Add three-quarters of the dressing to the bowl with the broccoli, and toss to combine. Taste, and add more dressing if you prefer, as well as additional salt or red pepper flakes, if needed.

RADICCHIO AND CHICKPEAS WITH CREAMY LEMON DRESSING

IN HER BOOK *BITTER*, JENNIFER MCLAGAN admits that "a reluctance to eat bitter foods is understandable, as we all have an innate aversion to bitter tastes." It's true that even the bitter lovers among us (a group I belong to) eat it with a sense of transgression, as if we know we are loving a taste on the outskirts of popular opinion.

I crave bitter flavors, and if I get my hands on a particularly good head of Belgian endive or radicchio, I often find myself eating it leaf by leaf at the counter, crunching away before I even start the recipe for which the green was intended. For me, it's not only the bitterness I love, but the more subtle inherently floral quality that always comes along with it. Smell as you take a bite, and the floral nature of the bitter is hard to ignore. This salad makes use of not only radicchio but also the tiny closed Belgian endive, another star of the bitter category. Creamy dressings are ideal for bitter greens, because they mellow out the bite but enhance the sweetness. If you don't have preserved lemon in your refrigerator, just use a teaspoon of fresh lemon zest.

SERVES 4 TO 6

DRESSING

⅓ cup crème fraîche or plain whole-milk yogurt

1½ tablespoons fresh lemon juice, plus more as needed

1½ tablespoons olive oil

1 tablespoon minced preserved lemon rind (see page 57) or 1 teaspoon fresh lemon zest

Freshly ground black pepper

SALAD

6 ounces radicchio (½ small head), roughly chopped

6 ounces butter lettuce (1 small head), torn

1 head of Belgian endive, leaves separated and cut into 1-inch slices

1 cup cooked chickpeas

⅓ cup golden raisins

Kosher salt

¼ cup toasted, chopped pecans (see page 136)

Freshly ground black pepper

1. Make the dressing: Combine the crème fraîche, lemon juice, olive oil, preserved lemon rind, and several grinds of pepper in a pint-sized jar. Cover the jar and shake vigorously to combine. Taste, and add more pepper or lemon juice, if you like. The dressing can be quite thick, but if it's not pourable, loosen it up with a little lemon juice or water.

(recipe continues)

2. Make the salad: Combine the radicchio, butter lettuce, and endive in a large bowl. Add about a third of the dressing and toss to coat the leaves. Taste and add more dressing, if needed. The leaves should be well coated but not soaked. Transfer the dressed leaves to a large, wide bowl or platter. Do not rinse out the bowl.

3. Add the chickpeas and raisins to the bowl and sprinkle them with a pinch of salt. Top with a dollop of dressing and gently stir to coat the chickpeas and raisins before adding them to the greens. Finish with the pecans, a final sprinkle of salt, and several grinds of pepper.

HOW TO TOAST NUTS

Toasting brings out the flavor in nuts, and I find a toasted nut is infinitely more delicious than a raw one. Toast a handful of nuts quickly in a dry skillet on the stove top, or roast your nuts and seeds in the oven. I toast most nuts at 350°F on an ungreased baking sheet just until they start to brown, 6 to 9 minutes. Seeds roast faster, in 4 to 6 minutes.

CUCUMBER SHISO SOBA

SHISO IS AN HERB WITH WIDE, SLIGHTLY furry leaves in dark purple and green. It's in the mint family, and it tastes somewhere between mint and basil with a little anise thrown in. You'll often find it in maki rolls with cucumber or avocado, and as it gets more popular, it shows up in everything from salads to simple syrup for cocktails. Here in this cold, summery, one-bowl dinner, it infuses smashed cucumbers and a tangy dressing. My friend Tara once said that soba was the sexiest noodle, and I think she's right—especially in this dish with so many shades of green. I've borrowed the smashing and pre-salting of the cucumbers from a traditional Chinese method of preparing them, and it creates a rough-edged quick pickle that really absorbs the flavors in the bowl. This is a good recipe for improvisation, whether you don't have all the ingredients or you just want to change it up. Can't find shiso? Use basil. No edamame? Try sugar snaps. And the avocado adds a nice creaminess and one more shade of green, but it's totally optional. Feel free to make this ahead of time. It's great on day one but really fantastic on day two, after the flavors have had a chance to come together.

SERVES 6

1½ pounds cucumbers (5 to 6 small or 1½ large)

1 tablespoon kosher salt, plus more for the pot

12 ounces soba

3 tablespoons rice vinegar

2 tablespoons Asian sesame oil

1 tablespoon olive oil

1½ tablespoons tamari or soy sauce

1 teaspoon sugar

½ teaspoon crushed red pepper flakes

2 cups frozen shelled edamame (1 12-ounce bag), thawed under cold running water

½ cup finely chopped fresh shiso leaves

2 scallions (white and light green parts), thinly sliced

¼ cup toasted sesame seeds

Optional: 1 avocado, cubed, for serving

1. Place the cucumbers on the counter, and use a rolling pin or big wooden spoon to whack the cucumbers until they split in several places. Quarter each smashed cucumber lengthwise, and cut each spear into ¾-inch pieces.

2. Transfer the cucumbers to a large colander. Massage the salt into the cucumbers, then weight them down with a plate and something heavy (a jar filled with water works well). Let the cucumbers drain for 15 minutes, then give them a light rinse under the faucet. This should wash off a bit, but not all, of the salt.

3. Meanwhile, bring a large pot of salted water to a boil over medium-high heat. Add the soba and cook, stirring occasionally, until tender, 4 to 5 minutes. Drain the soba and rinse repeatedly to cool the soba down completely.

4. Whisk together the rice vinegar, sesame oil, olive oil, tamari, sugar, and red pepper flakes in a large, wide bowl. Add the soba, edamame, cucumbers, shiso, scallions, and sesame seeds, tossing gently to coat the ingredients in the dressing. Serve with the avocado on the side, if using, and let each diner add it to their liking.

GRILLED SUMMER SQUASH WITH BASIL RICOTTA

OFTEN BY MIDSUMMER, YOU CAN FIND A green and yellow rainbow of wild and curvy summer squash keeping the straitlaced zucchini company. From the yellow crookneck to the striped summer green tiger, each squash has its own texture and flavor. My very favorite is the pale green pattypan squash. They're shaped like UFOs, and when sliced horizontally, the rounds look like flowers. They also are especially sweet, with a more floral quality than most summer squash. Grilling is one of the best ways to enjoy summer squash, as it firms up and caramelizes the outside while bringing out all the juice and flavor the meaty inside has to offer. This recipe is a great way to use several varieties at once. As long as you keep the slices about the same thickness, they'll cook similarly, and all the different shapes and colors look so lovely on the plate.

SERVES 4 TO 6

1 tablespoon balsamic vinegar
¼ cup plus 2 tablespoons olive oil, plus more for drizzling
1 tablespoon apple cider vinegar
1 tablespoon tamari or soy sauce
1½ teaspoons kosher salt
1½ pounds summer squash, cut lengthwise into ½-inch slices
8 ounces whole-milk ricotta
¼ cup finely chopped fresh basil
Zest and juice of ½ lemon
Optional: 1 tablespoon fresh summer savory or marjoram leaves

1. Combine the balsamic vinegar, the ¼ cup of olive oil, the apple cider vinegar, tamari, and the 1 teaspoon of salt in a jar, and shake to combine.

2. Use a fork to poke holes in the skin sides of the squash slices. Lay the squash out in a shallow baking dish and pour the marinade over it. Cover and let the squash sit for at least 30 minutes at room temperature, or transfer to the refrigerator for up to 8 hours.

3. Meanwhile, combine the ricotta, basil, lemon zest and juice, the remaining 2 tablespoons olive oil, and the ½ teaspoon of salt in a medium bowl.

4. Heat your grill until it's medium-hot.

5. Transfer the squash to the grill, draining off the excess marinade. Grill the squash until tender and golden, 3 to 5 minutes per side. Transfer to a platter.

6. Spoon the ricotta over the squash and top with the summer savory, if using, and a drizzle of olive oil.

FRESH CORN AND STONE FRUIT

THERE ARE SOME RECIPES THAT HAVE THE power to transform the way you conceive of yourself as a cook. At least that's how I went from someone who cooked out of necessity to someone who cooks well. You'd think these moments happen around the mastery of hard techniques in the kitchen, but I think it's the moments when we take ownership of the simple everyday skills that make the difference. How to salt an ingredient well, how to brown meat so it forms a golden crust and instantly releases from the pan, how to quickly chop a carrot into perfect, regular ovals—these skills have each bolstered my confidence and given me a little kick to move on, to learn more, and to feel good about my work in the kitchen.

This recipe is a prime example of one of those essential skills: how to courageously combine ingredients. The unexpected partnership of raw corn and stone fruit is perfect, and it's one of those ideal dishes that takes 5 minutes to put together and seems to surprise and delight everyone who eats it. A version of this recipe lives in my second book, and it is still, to date, one of my very favorite recipes. The concepts at work here— good produce combined in an unexpected but simple way to create something so much more than the sum of its parts—really were the inspiration for this whole book, and I had to bring this one back to take its place among these recipes. This is a broader form of the recipe, with more choices and a good level of heat from the jalapeño.

SERVES 4

4 or 5 ears of corn

2 ripe nectarines or peeled peaches, pitted and cut into bite-size pieces

¼ cup thinly sliced scallions (2 to 3 scallions, using all the white and half the green parts)

¼ cup thinly sliced fresh basil or roughly chopped fresh cilantro

½ teaspoon kosher salt

Freshly ground black pepper

1 jalapeño, seeded and finely chopped

2 tablespoons fresh lime juice (1 lime)

Husk the corn and then cut the kernels right into a serving bowl. (There's a simple tool that removes kernels without slicing them that I keep around just for corn season, but you can also use a knife, taking care not to cut directly through all the kernels.) Be sure to catch the corn milk in the bowl as well. Add the nectarines, scallions, basil, salt, several grinds of pepper, and the jalapeño to the bowl with the corn. Drizzle the lime juice over the salad and stir gently to combine.

MILLET-STUFFED TOMATOES

STUFFED VEGETABLES PLAYED A MAJOR role in my own childhood in the eighties. My grandparents were vegetarians, and stuffed vegetables had the ability to take the spotlight like a large piece of meat. No turkey for Thanksgiving? Stuff a butternut squash with rice and cranberries, and it's just as grand. Birthday dinner in August? Nothing says "special" like a gargantuan zucchini, left in the garden until it's big enough to hold an entire batch of corn bread and who knows what else. Honestly, I've had enough stuffed vegetables to last me a lifetime. I'm over it. Except, that is, when it comes to tomatoes. There's something about a stuffed tomato that makes me feel like a lady who lunches— it makes me sit up straighter and crave white wine with lunch. It's an exquisitely civilized dish and really good to boot. Tomatoes are traditionally stuffed with bread crumbs or rice, but I love them with millet. It's an underappreciated grain, quick cooking and nutty, and it stays just firm enough to give these tomatoes a structure.

You can make these with any variety or color of tomato, but it works best with nice round tomatoes. Try, if you can, to choose tomatoes of a similar size. Don't try to stuff huge, splitting heirlooms—save those for your tomato sandwich. These are wonderful cold on the second day, especially with a squeeze of lemon or a drizzle of vinaigrette.

SERVES 6

3 pounds tomatoes (about 6 medium)
Kosher salt
1 teaspoon finely minced garlic (1 clove)
2 tablespoons olive oil
½ cup packed fresh basil leaves, torn or cut into ribbons
½ cup packed fresh flat-leaf parsley leaves, roughly chopped
1⅓ cups millet
¾ cup grated Parmesan, pecorino, or Romano cheese

1. Carefully core each tomato with a paring knife, cutting it a bit wider than the core to create a round opening big enough to stuff, but small enough so the tomato doesn't entirely come apart. Use a spoon to scoop the pulp from each tomato, transferring and reserving it in a large measuring cup as you go. Scoop carefully so as to maintain the walls of each tomato. Set the tomatoes upright in a roasting pan or shallow Dutch oven that holds all the tomatoes snugly, propping them up against each other, and sprinkle the inside of each tomato with salt.

2. Preheat the oven to 375°F.

3. You should have 3 cups of tomato guts. If you're short of 3 cups, top it off with a bit of water. Pour this into a medium saucepan, using your hands to crush any large chunks of tomato. Add the garlic, 1 tablespoon of the

(recipe continues)

olive oil, ¼ teaspoon salt, about half of each of the herbs, and the millet to the saucepan with the tomato guts. Bring just to a boil, stirring constantly. Cover the pot, reduce the heat to medium low, and cook until the millet is tender and the liquid is absorbed, 25 to 30 minutes. Remove the pan from the heat. If the millet is cooked and there's still liquid in the pot, pour the millet through a strainer to remove the liquid—then return the millet to the pot.

4. Stir half of the remaining herbs along with ½ cup of the cheese into the cooked millet. Taste the mixture and adjust for salt. It should be tasty but not too salty. Spoon the millet mixture into the tomatoes, gently packing it down as you reach the top of each tomato. Don't worry if a tomato splits; just reshape it and prop it up against the others. Drizzle the remaining 1 tablespoon of olive oil over the tomatoes and cover the pan. (If the pan doesn't have a cover, use aluminum foil.)

5. Bake for 25 minutes, then remove the pan from the oven. Sprinkle the remaining cheese over the top of the tomatoes, and put the pan under the broiler just long enough to melt the cheese and add a little crunch to the millet. Finish with the reserved fresh herbs before serving.

TOMATO VARIETIES

If you are buying tomatoes at the grocery store, your choices are usually big red (the classic), small red (the cherry), or oval red (the paste). If it's August and you're lucky, there will be a bin vaguely labeled "heirlooms," a distinction that seems, in this case, to be reserved for oddly shaped, multicolored tomatoes with big splits down their seams. But there's more to it, of course. And when you buy tomatoes from a farmer who goes beyond big, small, and oval, navigating through the varieties can get a little daunting. Here's what you need to know.

Most supermarket tomatoes have been specifically bred to do well commercially. Because they've been refined and changed over time, they are known as *hybrids*. That perfect round, red tomato travels well, grows consistently, and looks good in the bin. You'll also see hybrid tomatoes at the farmers' market or farm stand, as most small-scale tomato farmers grow both hybrids and heirlooms. But perfect shape and color are no reasons to write off a tomato! At high-tomato season, a good ripe hybrid tomato carries just as much deliciousness as an heirloom.

Heirlooms are varieties that have been passed down from tomato generation to tomato generation, and they haven't been changed to make them more commercially viable. It's not an official agricultural term, so it's used pretty loosely and sometimes even as an excuse to charge more. Mostly what you know from the term is that you're getting a "true," unaltered variety and that presumably the seeds have been saved from year to year. Because heirlooms have not been bred for commercial success, they often don't travel well, are shaped irregularly, and are often different colors, but some regular round and red tomatoes are heirloom varieties, too.

Try to buy tomatoes that are the size you will eat in one sitting. A gigantic heirloom might be beautiful, but if you have a single tomato sandwich planned, the rest of the tomato might go to waste. If you do use just part of a tomato, place the unused portion cut-side down on a plate and use the rest within a day.

Tomatoes are ripe when they really give at the press of your finger. Don't be afraid of large splits in big tomatoes—just cut them out with a paring knife. Set unripe tomatoes upside down on the windowsill. And remember, never refrigerate your tomatoes.

You'll see many different kinds of tomatoes at the store or farmers' market, but let's group them into shapes and colors to discuss their best uses.

CHERRY TOMATOES are little and extra sweet. Look for classics like the Supersweet 100, or, perhaps the sweetest of them all, the bright orange Sungolds. The Black Cherry, an heirloom cultivar, is a deep purple and slightly larger and richer in flavor than the average cherry tomato. Cherries are best for snacking, for slicing in half and adding to grain and vegetable salads, or for roasting. Because they're so small, roasted cherry tomatoes can be spread on bread, almost like a preserve. Grape tomatoes are a bit larger than cherries but share many of the same qualities.

PASTE TOMATOES are small and oval. They're good for slicing but are most prized for making sauce and salsa because they're easy to seed, have a drier flesh that cooks down well, and they don't have much juice. Look for Roma, Juliet, and San Marzano varieties. These are also great for roasting.

GREEN TOMATOES tend to be lower in sugar, so the tang of the tomato really comes through. Look for the stripy Green Zebra or the grassy Cherokee Green. Don't confuse these with unripe green tomatoes—these are completely green even at their peak ripeness. Green tomatoes are best raw, as their green color becomes pale brown when roasted or cooked into a sauce.

YELLOW TOMATOES are low in acid, so they tend to have the mellowest flavor. They're not a good choice for canning, as the low acid messes with the predictable pH you need to can safely. As with green tomatoes, I think yellow tomatoes are best raw. Look for the Yellow Brandywine and the pale yellow Great White.

RED AND PINK TOMATOES are high in acid and sweetness. They're a good choice for eating raw, roasting, or turning into sauce, as they maintain a good red color when cooked. Look for Brandywines and Big Beefs.

PURPLE AND BLACK TOMATOES are some of my favorites. They tend to have a deeper, richer flavor while still maintaining a good acid level. These are good for eating raw and for cooking. Look for the Cherokee Purple and Black Krim.

CAPRESE

MOMENTS BEFORE I HAD TO COMMIT TO a recipe list for this book, I was on a dock in Westport, Massachusetts, with my friend Mary Natalizia. Mary is an amazing cook, especially when it comes to doing simple things better than you ever thought they could be. I was struggling with the decision of which raw tomato recipe to include in this chapter. The best tomato sandwich? Fresh tomatoes with pasta and balsamic vinegar? If I really had to decide on my favorite way to eat a good tomato, it would probably be whole with salt and pepper. But that doesn't quite make it into recipe territory. But then there was the caprese: standard mediocre wedding-buffet fare, ideal picnic food, and a perfectly acceptable dinner on any in-season evening. That being said, it's been done. But when I brought up the challenge of the perfect tomato recipe, Mary answered with a question.

"Wouldn't you eat the caprese every single day when the tomatoes and basil are good?"

"More than once a day," I admitted.

The caprese that followed that conversation confirmed it, and it also convinced me I should always do it Mary's way. She insists that both the cheese and the basil should be torn, not cut, the olive oil go directly on each tomato, and the salad always sit at room temperature for 30 minutes before it goes on the table to let the vinegar (always red wine, never balsamic) do its magic.

Mary serves this with a loaf of Italian bread, torn into large pieces to soak up the dressing, and after having it that way, I always will, too.

SERVES 4

2 pounds ripe tomatoes (any size or variety larger than a cherry tomato)
½ teaspoon kosher salt
8 ounces fresh mozzarella
3 tablespoons olive oil
2 tablespoons red wine vinegar
Freshly ground black pepper
20 fresh basil leaves
For serving: Torn Italian bread

1. Core the tomatoes and slice them into manageable pieces that can easily be transported with a serving spoon. Small tomatoes can be halved lengthwise and then cut into ½-inch slices, but larger tomatoes should be quartered before slicing. Lay the tomatoes out on a large platter, and sprinkle them with ¼ teaspoon of the salt.

2. Tear the mozzarella into bite-sized pieces, and tuck them in and around the tomatoes. Drizzle with the olive oil, taking care to get a bit directly on each tomato. Drizzle with the vinegar, and sprinkle with the remaining salt and lots of pepper. Top the whole platter with the basil leaves, tearing each leaf into three or four pieces as you go. Let the salad sit for 30 minutes before serving. Allow people to serve themselves from the tray, but keep the serving tray within reach so everyone can sop up the dressing with the bread.

TOMATO CHEDDAR PIE

I THINK THE PASSAGE OF TIME IN THE summer can really be measured by the preciousness of each tomato. In the beginning, tomatoes that have never seen the outside of the greenhouse show up, six bucks a pound, and we buy one with a clear image of the tomato sandwich it will become. Later they get better, cheaper, and split down the middle, and we can buy bags of them for fresh tomato sauce or big trays of roasted tomatoes. Finally, they get thick and woolly, saved on the counter from the first frost that did or did not come. Those tomatoes never get very good, but we eat them out of some sense of responsibility to our future January selves who would kill for a half-ripe September tomato.

Laurie Colwin wrote about a tomato pie in her essay "Tomatoes" that originally got the idea of tomato pie stuck in my head. Her recipe, borrowed from a teahouse not far from my hometown, was the seed of this tomato Cheddar pie. This is best made when the tomatoes are good and as plentiful as zucchini, and when the extravagant quantity of basil should also be easy to come by. The pie is juicy, and although the crust does a great job of soaking up most of the tomato-basil nectar, there will definitely be liquid left in the pie pan. Spoon it up and enjoy it—it's the best part.

**MAKES ONE 9-INCH PIE,
PLUS 1 EXTRA PIE CRUST**

CRUST

2 cups all-purpose flour, plus more for rolling

¼ cup spelt or whole-wheat pastry flour

1 cup (2 sticks) cold unsalted butter, cut into small pieces, plus more for greasing the dish

⅓ cup cold water

2 teaspoons apple cider vinegar

½ teaspoon kosher salt

FILLING

2 cups (8 ounces) grated sharp Cheddar cheese

1¼ pounds tomatoes, halved through the stem and thinly sliced at a 90-degree angle

1 cup loosely packed basil leaves, torn or chopped into ribbons

Kosher salt and freshly ground black pepper

1 tablespoon finely minced garlic (2 to 4 cloves)

1. Make the crust: Combine the flours and butter in the bowl of a stand mixer, using your hands to coat the butter in the flour. Put the bowl in the refrigerator. Combine the water, vinegar, and salt in a measuring cup, stirring to dissolve the salt. Put the mixture in the freezer for 10 minutes.

2. Remove the mixtures from the refrigerator and freezer. Using the paddle attachment, blend the flour mixture on low speed until it has the texture of crumbly meal. With the

(recipe continues)

mixer still running, slowly pour in the water mixture. The dough will be crumbly at first, then after 10 or 20 seconds, it will come together in a ball. Stop the mixer. Turn the dough out onto the counter, and divide it into 2 disks, each about 1 inch thick. Wrap each disk in waxed paper or plastic wrap, and refrigerate for at least 1 hour and up to 3 days. You'll only use one crust for this pie, so the other disk can go straight into the freezer, if you don't have other pie plans for the week.

3. Remove one disk of pastry from the refrigerator. Grease a 9-inch freezer-to-oven pie dish (Pyrex, stainless steel, or most stoneware) with butter. Unwrap the disk, place it on a lightly floured counter, and, starting from the center, roll the dough into a circle 12 to 14 inches in diameter and ⅛ inch thick. To transfer the crust, fold it in half, then fold that semicircle in half again so that you have a quarter of a circle. Line up the corner of the quarter with the center of your pie dish, and unfold the quarter back into a semicircle, then into the full circle. Trim off any errant edges to

create an overhang of about 1 inch. Fold the overhang under the edge, and use your hands or a fork to crimp the crust. Freeze the crust for at least 1 hour and up to 3 days. (If you freeze the crust for longer than an hour or two, cover it with plastic wrap.)

4. Preheat the oven to 375°F. Place a baking sheet in the center of the oven.

5. Remove the crust from the freezer. Scatter a small handful of cheese over the bottom of the crust. Layer on half the tomatoes, followed by half the basil. Sprinkle with salt, pepper, and the minced garlic. Now add half of the remaining cheese, followed by the other half of the basil, and the remaining tomatoes. Sprinkle with salt and pepper again, and top with the last of the Cheddar. Put the pie on the baking sheet.

6. Bake until the crust is golden and the filling begins to bubble, 55 minutes to 1 hour. Let the pie sit for at least 15 minutes before cutting into it.

ROASTED TOMATO PANZANELLA

I DIDN'T GROW UP IN A FAMILY THAT DID much preserving, so it wasn't until I started working at the farmers' market that I adjusted my idea of tomato quantity from singles to *cases*. The first time I had a kitchen full of tomatoes ripe to bursting, I canned the whole lot of them. The seeds! The mess! The skins! It was not a positive experience. And although I've grown more comfortable with tomato canning over the years, I'll always choose roasting and freezing when I have the chance. Here's how it works: Cut tomatoes in half or in quarters. Lay them on parchment-lined trays. Sprinkle with olive oil, salt, and herbs, and roast in a 250°F oven *forever,* that is, 1 to 2 hours for cherry or grape tomatoes and up to 4 or 5 hours for larger tomatoes. This method creates trays full of outrageously delicious tomato gold: sugary caramelized bits, tomato juice and herb-infused oil, and roasted tomato pulp that will improve the flavor of endless recipes in the kitchen. I tip the full contents of each tray into a freezer bag and stack them in the freezer. The bags get opened throughout the year to thaw and become tomato sauce, soup, and anything that calls for canned tomatoes.

Tomatoes will roast almost as well at higher temps if you're in a hurry, so I've upped the heat to speed this recipe along. Roasted cherry tomatoes really make this late-summer salad special, and the deep red against the kale is gorgeous. If you have different varieties and colors of small tomatoes, even better. All of the components in this salad can be made up to 2 days ahead of time.

SERVES 4

2 pints cherry or grape tomatoes (about 1½ pounds)
Kosher salt
5½ tablespoons olive oil
2 tablespoons balsamic vinegar
1 medium garlic clove, crushed into a paste with the side of a knife or a garlic press
Freshly ground black pepper
½ loaf rustic sourdough or ciabatta bread (about 8 ounces), torn into large bites
1 large bunch kale (about 8 ounces), stems removed, leaves torn or chopped
4 ounces feta cheese, crumbled or cubed

1. Preheat the oven to 325°F. Line a rimmed baking sheet with parchment paper.

2. Cut each cherry tomato in half lengthwise and line them up on the prepared baking sheet, skin-side down. Sprinkle with salt and drizzle with 1 tablespoon of the olive oil. Roast until they begin to collapse, about 50 minutes.

3. Meanwhile, combine 3 tablespoons of the olive oil with the balsamic vinegar and garlic paste in a small jar. Add ¼ teaspoon salt and several grinds of pepper. Close the jar and shake to combine.

4. Prepare the bread. Heat 1½ tablespoons of olive oil in a large skillet set over medium-high heat. Add the bread and fry, stirring often, until the edges crisp up and begin to color, 3 to 4 minutes. Remove from the heat.

5. Combine the kale, bread, and feta in a large bowl. Add half of the dressing and toss to combine. Taste and add more dressing, if desired. Gently fold in the tomatoes and any liquid on the tray. Top with salt and pepper.

EGGPLANT DENGAKU

MY GRANDMOTHER PASSED DOWN TO ME her inability to eat eggplant (she never hesitated to tell people how it just didn't agree with her), but that hasn't stopped me from developing a deep admiration for the vegetable from afar.

Over the years at the farmers' market, I've developed what I can only describe as a crush. The eggplants show up in their bins, and I start to gush about the depth of the inky color and the curves of each fruit. Although I don't get to eat it, I do know that eggplant has a singular ability to hold its shape and meatiness under heat. It's often compared with zucchini, but it doesn't weep liquid or go mushy, and the flavor of the cooked eggplant is far more rich and complex than a zucchini or summer squash.

You'll probably find the most common eggplants: classically voluptuous large oval fruits from dark purple to black in color. Smaller Asian varieties, often with fuchsia-and-white-striped skin, are becoming more popular, too. These slender little purple eggplants are so beautiful that it's a shame to chop them up. I always suggest grilling them instead, so you don't lose out on that curve and color.

Lissa McGovern, my very dear friend and dedicated recipe tester, is a lover and master of eggplant. I asked her to contribute an eggplant recipe to this book, as I couldn't supply one, and she re-created the traditional Japanese eggplant dish *nasu dengaku*. The sauce is also great on grilled tofu.

SERVES 4

4 small Asian eggplants, halved lengthwise
1 tablespoon olive oil

SAUCE
¼ cup red miso paste
2 tablespoons mirin
2 tablespoons sake
2 tablespoons maple syrup
1 teaspoon grated fresh ginger

For serving: 2 scallions (white and light green parts), thinly sliced

1. Grill the eggplant: Heat your grill to medium-high heat. Use a knife to score the cut side of each eggplant half, then brush the flesh with the olive oil. Grill, cut-side down, for 10 minutes. Flip the eggplants and grill on the skin side until the whole eggplant is browned and tender, 5 to 10 minutes more.

2. Make the sauce: Combine the miso, mirin, and sake in a small saucepan set over medium heat. Bring to a boil, stirring constantly, and cook, stirring often, for about 2 minutes. Add the maple syrup and cook, continuing to stir, until the whole mixture gets quite thick, 1 to 2 minutes. Remove the pan from the heat, and stir in the ginger.

3. When the eggplant is ready, transfer it to a platter, cut-side up. Spoon the sauce over each eggplant, and top with scallions.

POBLANO
RAJAS TACOS

WHEN WE NEED REALLY GOOD TACOS, WE drive nearly halfway across Massachusetts to Mission Cantina in Amherst. It's in a strange pocket of town, surrounded by condos and cornfields, and you have to be careful not to drink too many Mexican beers because there's nowhere to walk them off before you get back in the car. But the tacos are the best I've had in New England—definitely worth the drive.

It was there that I first tried poblano rajas tacos. It's the vegetarian option on their taco list, and I've come to love it more than any other. Strips (*rajas*) of pepper are the star here, and they're meaty enough to hold up to the tortilla. They're deep and smoky and need very little accompaniment. Except Mexican beer, of course. I like to roast peppers in my oven, but if you're eager to grill or it's already going, you can roast them on a hot grill instead.

MAKES ABOUT 10 TACOS

1 pound poblano peppers (about 6)

Neutral oil, such as grapeseed or sunflower

1 teaspoon whole cumin seeds

1 medium onion, halved vertically and sliced thin into ribbons

1 tablespoon fresh oregano or 1 teaspoon dried

Kosher salt

10 small corn tortillas

For serving: Sour cream or crème fraîche, soft cheese (such as Cotija, chèvre, or mild feta), Simplest Slaw (page 59), lime wedges

1. Set your broiler rack about 6 inches from the broiler element. Preheat it to medium, or if your broiler has a temperature setting, 450°F. Line a rimmed baking sheet with aluminum foil.

2. Lightly rub each pepper with oil, laying them on the prepared baking sheet as you go. Broil until the peppers are blackened on all sides, turning them a few times over the course of cooking, anywhere from 7 to 15 minutes per side. Stay attentive to their progress; the peppers are done when they're mostly blistered and collapsed. Use tongs to transfer them to a big heatproof bowl. Cover tightly with plastic wrap or a plate that fits the bowl exactly. Let sit for about 20 minutes.

3. After they "sweat," the peppers should slide right out of their skins. Put on rubber gloves to protect your hands from the heat of

(recipe continues)

the peppers. Separate the stems, skin, and seeds from the flesh of the peppers, laying the peppers on a cutting board as you go. Slice the peppers into long strips.

4. Heat about 1 tablespoon oil in a medium skillet over medium-high heat. When it shimmers, add the cumin seeds. Cook for a few seconds, then add the onion and cook, stirring constantly, until the onion wilts and chars, 4 to 5 minutes. Add the peppers and oregano, and cook, stirring constantly, until they're tender and browned in spots, 3 to 5 minutes. Remove the pan from the heat and salt the peppers to taste.

5. Heat a separate skillet over medium heat. Warm the tortillas in the skillet one or two at a time, stacking them on a plate as you go. Serve the poblanos on the tortillas, topped with the sour cream, cheese, and slaw, with the lime wedges on the side.

MELON WITH ARUGULA AND PROSCIUTTO

OVER THE FOUR YEARS I LIVED IN SANTA Fe throughout college, I spent a lot of time at the farmers' market. The Santa Fe market was well established even then, active since the sixties and even boasting a few years during the nineties with Deborah Madison as manager. I loved the market most because it was a gallery of the differences between that home and the one I'd come from. I'd grown up in the land of apples, tomatoes, and blueberries, but in Santa Fe, the stars were the chiles, beans, lavender, and melons. Later in the summer, there was a farmer who'd drive right into the market and sell melons out of the back of his truck. They were piled like river rocks of different shapes and patterns, mysterious varieties like Jake's and Crenshaw that you had to taste to understand. I had to walk a mile home from the market in the heat, but I'd always buy a melon, because every melon I ate that summer surpassed the previous one as the best thing I'd ever tasted.

Mediocre melon is edible. Supermarket cantaloupe in April is passable, and we often buy melons throughout the year. But a truly great melon will make you close your eyes and stop everything. Hand me a spoon and I'll eat a half a melon on my own. But if we need a recipe, I prefer something with a little savory, a little salt, and a little green to prop that melon up on a pedestal of other flavors. Somehow all that contrast just makes it that much sweeter. Eat this all right away; it doesn't keep well.

SERVES 4

1 tablespoon fresh lemon juice
2 tablespoons olive oil
¼ teaspoon kosher salt
8 ounces arugula, roughly chopped
½ cantaloupe, honeydew, or other ripe melon, peeled, seeded, and cut into rough ½-inch pieces
2 ounces chèvre
3 ounces thinly sliced prosciutto, torn into thin strips
Freshly ground black pepper

Stir together the lemon juice, olive oil, and salt in a large bowl. Add the arugula and melon, and toss gently to coat everything in the dressing. Use your hands or a fork to evenly distribute the chèvre over the salad. Top with the prosciutto and lots of ground pepper.

WARMTH
AND
COMFORT

THERE'S ALWAYS A SHIFT IN LATE AUGUST. IT COULD BE A FULL MONTH before the end of summer, but nonetheless, something changes. I'll be walking the dog through the field beyond our house, and, where once was uninterrupted warm air, there are pockets of cold, suspended in mysterious places as if the field were made of water. The mist comes back in the mornings, and I need to grab a sweater if we're going to eat dinner outside. And when the cold comes back, the shape of my cooking changes.

Tastes are quieter in the winter. In the summer, food tastes like the sun and the ground and simply *itself*. Other flavors exist to bring out the earth in the beet, the sweetness of the tomato, the floral bitter of the green. But in the winter, the tastes shift. Often I'll be working with stored produce or vegetables that have traveled, and the flavors might have mellowed. It becomes more exciting to combine flavors, to pump the spices, to cook with stock and wine and cream. And by the time we're in January and February, dinners become an event—the only thing to look forward to in a world of cold and ice and quiet. I make small, rich meals that include the salads of winter: kale, endive, watermelon radish. So this chapter reflects this change in season and flavor, and you'll find not only comforting food for cold weather but the fresh and crunchy salads that complement them. In some ways, the cold weather is the very best time for salads, because a little bit of freshness is the answer to all that we're missing. Pair a good winter salad with a dish full of cream and comfort, and you've got my favorite dinner.

GARLICKY
KOHLRABI
WITH DANDELION
AND CHICKPEAS

WHEN YOU SAUTÉ KOHLRABI, THE MOIS-ture concentrates in the middle, and it becomes juicy like a water chestnut. I had initially only roasted it into fries (page 58) or eaten it raw, so the first time I ate it like this, combined with greens and chickpeas, was at my friend Richard's house. I went back for seconds and thirds, and as a reward, he went out into his garden and brought me back a kohlrabi the size of my head. I'd never seen one that large, but it was perfect all the way through, sweet and crisp and never woody. We ate that single kohlrabi for days, and it gave me a perfect opportunity to play around with the sweet and bitter flavors I'd loved at Richard's house.

This is a great hearty side dish, especially wonderful alongside fish. Or serve it over a grain, and it becomes a simple meal on its own.

SERVES 4

2 tablespoons olive oil
1½ pounds green or purple kohlrabi (about 3 medium kohlrabi), peeled and cut into ½-inch chunks
½ teaspoon kosher salt
1 bunch dandelion greens (about 8 ounces), rinsed and roughly chopped
¼ cup water
1 tablespoon minced garlic (2 to 3 cloves)
1 cup cooked chickpeas
Large flake sea salt, such as Maldon
Freshly ground black pepper

1. Heat 1 tablespoon of the oil in a large sauté or frying pan set over medium-high heat. Add the kohlrabi and cook, stirring often but not constantly, until it colors on all sides, 8 to 10 minutes. Sprinkle the kohlrabi with the kosher salt.

2. Add the dandelion greens and water. Cover the pan, and let the mixture cook, stirring occasionally, until the greens are fully wilted, about 3 minutes. Uncover the pan, add the garlic and chickpeas, and continue to cook, stirring constantly, until the water evaporates, 2 to 3 minutes. Remove the pan from the heat. Top with the remaining 1 tablespoon of olive oil, the large flake salt, and plenty of pepper.

POLENTA WITH
ALL THE GREENS

THERE IS A MOMENT AS WE COME INTO FALL when I end up with a serious greens problem. Whereas the bounty in my kitchen once lived on the counter in the form of piles of USE-ME-RIGHT-NOW tomatoes and melons, now we are into the sweet frost-kissed kale and the flowering broccoli raab. Now there are so many beets, each bunch crowned with red-ribbed leaves, as well as kohlrabi and turnip greens, Swiss chard and spicy mustards—all shoved into the fridge precariously, one on top of the other, squeezed between the beer and the yogurt and the leftovers. There are days that I come home from working at the market with bags and bags of them. I don't want to compost good food, and I'm sure I'll think of *some* way to use all these greens.

This super-simple and adaptable dish is the solution. It cooks down and makes use of a large quantity of greens, and the more kinds you combine, the better. This also makes a great breakfast, and I won't argue if you fry an egg for the very top. I also love to give pasta this treatment—I cook the greens the same way and stir them into fettuccine.

If you're not yet an anchovy lover, I urge you not to let that ingredient scare you away here. They are very mellow and contribute a rich saltiness that's hard to identify. I like to buy my anchovies in large round jars packed in oil. They last a long time in the pantry, and the salty oil is a bonus ingredient.

SERVES 4 TO 6

7 cups water

1½ cups polenta

Kosher salt

3 to 4 bunches hearty greens (kale, Swiss chard, beet or turnip greens, kohlrabi greens, etc.), stemmed if necessary, roughly chopped

3 tablespoons unsalted butter

8 to 10 olive-oil-packed anchovies, rinsed and finely chopped

Optional: ⅛ teaspoon crushed red pepper flakes

¾ cup panko or rough homemade bread crumbs

1 tablespoon finely minced garlic (2 to 3 cloves)

2 tablespoons olive oil

¾ cup grated Parmesan cheese

Freshly ground black pepper

1. Bring 6 cups of the water to a boil in a medium pot. Add the polenta and 1½ teaspoons salt, stirring gently to distribute the grains through the water. Reduce the heat to medium-low and cover the pot. Cook, stirring occasionally, until the polenta loses its graininess, 35 to 40 minutes. The polenta will get thicker toward the end of the cooking time, so add the remaining cup of water gradually over the last 10 minutes.

2. While the polenta cooks, bring a second large pot of salted water to a boil over high heat. Add the greens, bring the water back to a boil, reduce the heat to medium, and cook, stirring often, until the greens are tender, 3 to 5 minutes. Scoop out 1 cup of cooking water, then drain the greens in a colander. Return the pot to the stove.

3. Melt the butter in the pot set over medium heat. Add the anchovies and cook, stirring often, for about 1 minute. Add the red pepper flakes, if using, and reduce the heat to medium-low.

4. Add the bread crumbs to the anchovies and let them toast, stirring often, until they turn golden and soak up any remaining butter, about 2 minutes. Add the garlic and cook for 1 minute, stirring often to prevent the bread crumbs from burning. Transfer the bread-crumb mixture to a small bowl and return the pot to medium heat.

5. Return the drained greens to the pot. Stir in the olive oil, three-quarters of the Parmesan, three-quarters of the bread-crumb mixture, lots of fresh pepper, and a splash of the greens' cooking water.

6. Spoon the polenta into a large wide bowl or individual serving bowls and top with the remaining Parmesan. Spoon the greens over the polenta, and sprinkle the remaining bread-crumb mixture over the top.

CARAMELIZED FENNEL WITH CITRUS AND RICOTTA

TOWARD THE END OF MY WORK ON *THE Homemade Kitchen,* I spent a week in the Catskills at the Spruceton Inn. The innkeepers had recently bought the property, a field down a dirt road with two buildings: a house for them to live in and a nine-room classic motel. Casey and Steven are artists who, in addition to creating a getaway for city dwellers, wanted also to invite artists to come and work undisturbed.

I was one of their first artists in residence during the coldest March week I can remember. The mud froze in deep grooves, and the wind whipped around the motel. I wrote from morning until night, and I cooked all my meals on a one-burner stove in the corner of my simple room. I loved it. After over a decade of cooking for a family, a week of cooking exactly what I wanted *when* I wanted felt like a gift in itself, and it was a perfect opportunity to start dreaming of a vegetable book.

I made versions of this salad a few times over the course of that week, and I made it for Casey on my last day at the inn. I was so excited to have company in my room, and I put that tiny stove to work and filled the table with a real proper lunch. This is so simple and yet fancy. The combination of sweet, caramelized fennel, puckery citrus, and creamy ricotta is fresh and alive in a season of stored roots and hearty greens. You can play with whatever citrus is available to you—blood oranges, pomelos, or anything sweet and tangy would be wonderful.

SERVES 4 TO 6

3 tablespoons unsalted butter
2 medium fennel bulbs (about 1½ pounds), trimmed, cored, and thinly sliced lengthwise
2 tablespoons sugar
2 tablespoons fresh lemon juice (1 lemon)
1 grapefruit
1 orange
1 cup whole-milk ricotta
¼ cup thinly sliced fresh mint leaves
Kosher salt
Freshly ground black pepper

1. Melt the butter in a large skillet set over medium-high heat. Add the fennel in as close to a single layer as possible; a little overlap is fine. Cover the pan and cook, flipping once or twice, until the fennel is fork-tender and golden, about 10 minutes. Sprinkle the sugar over the fennel and let it cook undisturbed until it makes a caramel, about 2 minutes. Remove the pan from the heat and add the lemon juice. Scrape the fennel and all its sauce onto a platter.

2. While the fennel cooks, section, or supreme, the grapefruit and orange. If you can do this with the fruit in one hand and the knife in the other, cut it right over the platter with the fennel. Otherwise, do your best to trap the juice on a cutting board and add the juice to the platter as you go. To supreme the citrus, slice off the top and bottom poles with a paring knife. Then carefully cut the peel off the fruit from the top to the bottom, removing as much of the pith as possible. Cut along the membranes of the fruit to remove the inner flesh, separating each section and removing any seeds as you go. Layer the fruit over the fennel. Top with generous spoonfuls of ricotta and mint, and season with salt and pepper.

SHREDDED BRUSSELS WITH CRISPY SHALLOTS AND PECANS

ROASTED BRUSSELS SPROUTS HAVE ALWAYS been very hit or miss for me. Sometimes they're so good I want to eat the whole pan. But other times I get my heat or timing wrong, and the sprouts go mushy in the center.

Over the years I've moved on to other methods, and I don't miss roasting one bit. I love to simply halve and panfry them (see page 77), or shred and fry them in a hot pan, which is probably my favorite method. Here, I toss them with deep-fried shallots, shallot oil, and pecans, which makes a dish worthy of special meals. If you have a food processor, the Brussels sprouts prep is a breeze; otherwise, wait to make this until you have a friend in the kitchen looking for a task. Chopping those little sprouts one by one is a bit of a project.

This recipe gets much of its crunch and texture from deep-fried shallot rings, which are easy to make and a great addition to all sorts of dishes. Be sure to start the shallots out in cold oil and heat them up together to prevent burning. Use the leftover shallot oil in dressings or to add a shallot essence to meat or vegetables.

SERVES 4 TO 6

1 cup peanut or corn oil
¾ cup thinly sliced shallot rings (from 3 to 4 ounces shallots)
1 pound Brussels sprouts
⅓ cup pecans
¾ teaspoon kosher salt
Squeeze of lemon
Freshly ground black pepper

1. Pour the oil into a small skillet. Add the shallots, set the pan over medium heat, and cook, stirring frequently, until the shallots become golden, 11 to 13 minutes. Use a slotted spoon or skimmer to transfer the shallots to a paper-towel-lined plate. They'll crisp up as they cool. Leave the shallot oil in the skillet.

2. Trim away the bottoms of the sprouts and remove any brown or wilted outer leaves. Pass the Brussels sprouts through the grating disk of a food processor, or thinly slice the sprouts with a knife.

3. Set a large skillet or sauté pan over medium heat. Toast the pecans in the skillet, stirring often and taking care not to let them burn, until they barely color and smell nutty, 3 to 4 minutes. Transfer the pecans to a cutting board and roughly chop them.

(recipe continues)

4. Return the large skillet to medium-high heat. Spoon 2 tablespoons of the shallot oil into the large skillet. (Strain the rest and store it in your pantry for up to 1 month; use it on meats and vegetables.) Add the shredded Brussels sprouts and cook, stirring often, until they're bright green with crispy bits, 6 to 8 minutes. Add the salt as they cook, tossing to combine. Remove the pan from the heat and gently fold in the pecans. Transfer the Brussels sprouts to a platter and top with a generous squeeze of lemon, pepper, and the crispy shallots.

SAUSAGE AND SWISS CHARD STRATA

I STARTED MAKING SAVORY BREAD PUD-dings right around the time I started making bread. The bread felt so precious that I didn't want to lose a bit of it. Now I keep a bag in my freezer for ends and other lost bits, and those are saved for bread crumbs, bread puddings, and stratas. I love the combination here: salty sausage, grassy chard, creamy ricotta, and sour rye. It's a perfect hearty dinner—and a good brunch, too.

The sausage contributes quite a bit to the flavor here, so choose your own adventure. A plain and mellow sausage is good, but a spicy andouille will make it pop, or a sweet apple sausage will push it almost to the dessert side. Also, a note on salt and pepper: The flavor of this pudding varies greatly, depending on the flavor of the bread, sausage, and ricotta. I find it doesn't usually need any additional salt besides what's in the ingredients, but if one of your components is more bland, you might want to add a bit. Serve with salt and pepper alongside, too, so each diner can do as he or she pleases.

SERVES 6 TO 8

1 tablespoon unsalted butter, plus more for greasing the dish

1 pound (6 to 7 cups) cubed, day-old rye bread (rye sourdough is especially nice here)

3 cups whole milk

3 large eggs

2 cups chopped onions (about 2 onions)

8 cups (packed) washed, roughly chopped Swiss chard (1 to 2 bunches), stems and leaves separated

¼ cup water

12 ounces cooked sausage, cut into ½-inch-thick half-moons

1 cup whole-milk ricotta cheese (about 8 ounces)

½ cup grated Parmesan cheese

1. Preheat the oven to 375°F. Grease a 9 × 13-inch baking dish or equivalent casserole with butter.

2. Scatter the bread into the prepared dish. Whisk together the milk and eggs in a large bowl, and pour the milk mixture over the bread to soak while you cook the vegetables.

(recipe continues)

3. Melt the 1 tablespoon of butter in a large skillet set over medium heat. Add the onions and cook, stirring often, until soft, about 6 minutes. Add the Swiss chard stems and cook, stirring, until the stems are tender, 3 to 5 minutes. Add the Swiss chard leaves and water to the skillet. Bring to a boil, cover, and reduce the heat to medium-low. Cook, lifting the lid to toss the greens once or twice, until the greens are wilted but still bright green, 2 more minutes. Drain off any liquid from the skillet.

4. Fold the sausage, ricotta, half of the Parmesan, and the cooked greens into the bread mixture. Top with the remaining Parmesan.

5. Bake, uncovered, until the center doesn't weep when pierced with a knife, about 1 hour.

LEEK CARBONARA

THERE ARE A FEW ESSENTIAL THINGS I always try to keep in the house that make me feel like I have everything covered. I always need to have a few extra rolls of toilet paper and a full bottle of dishwashing liquid under the sink. When it comes to groceries, I try to shop so carbonara is always an option, no matter the circumstances—it's saved dinnertime on more occasions than I can count. I love to add a vegetable to the perfect mix of bacon, pasta, and egg to make it a one-bowl dinner. Greens, asparagus, even tomatoes have been great, but this one is a favorite, with long strings of sweet boiled leek tangled in with the pasta. It makes the whole dish lighter, sweeter, and so lovely to look at. Leeks are often used as a base for other dishes, but this recipe gives them their own moment. When you boil them, they turn a bright grassy green, and the root is tender and delicious all the way through. Try to have all of your ingredients ready to go when you begin, as this dish comes together all at once.

SERVES 4

Kosher salt

4 ounces slab or sliced bacon (4 to 6 slices), cut into ¼-inch pieces

2 large leeks

Vinegar

12 ounces dried spaghetti, fettuccine, or linguine

2 tablespoons unsalted butter

½ cup grated Parmesan cheese, plus more for sprinkling

¼ cup roughly chopped fresh tarragon

4 large eggs

Freshly ground black pepper

1. Bring a large pot of salted water to a boil over high heat. Simultaneously, heat your largest skillet or frying pan over medium-high heat. Fry the bacon in the skillet, stirring often, until it's crispy, 3 to 5 minutes. Use a slotted spoon to transfer the bacon to a small bowl. Leave the bacon fat in the pan and set aside.

2. Trim the root and the toughest green top from the leeks. (This will vary by leek, but tends to be about 3 inches from the top of each leek.) Cut each leek lengthwise in half, then in half again, repeating this until you have long, spaghetti-like slices of leek. Transfer the leeks to a bowl, cover with water, and add a splash of vinegar to help remove the dirt from the leeks. Let them sit for a few minutes and drain, giving them a rinse to make sure there's no remaining dirt.

3. When the water boils, add the pasta. Cook for about 5 minutes, then add the leeks. Continue to cook until the pasta is tender and the leeks are bright green, 3 to 4 more minutes. Pour a few cups of the pasta water into a smaller pot set over medium-low heat (you'll use this to poach the eggs), then drain the pasta and leeks in a colander.

4. Return the reserved skillet of bacon fat to medium-high heat. Add the butter, then whisk in about ½ cup of the reserved pasta cooking water. Add the pasta, leeks, Parmesan, cooked bacon, and three-quarters of the tarragon to the skillet, gently tossing until the pasta and leeks are fully coated in the sauce. Divide the pasta evenly among four plates or bowls.

5. Crack an egg into a ramekin or teacup. Pour off the most watery part of the white and give the small pot of reserved pasta-cooking water a little swirl to get the water moving. Gently slide the egg into the water and cook until the white is firm, 2½ minutes. Use a slotted spoon to lay the egg over one of the bowls of pasta. Repeat with the remaining 3 eggs. Top with the rest of the tarragon, lots of pepper, and a bit of extra Parmesan.

ROASTED RADISHES WITH FETA MINT SAUCE

ROASTED RADISHES ARE SURPRISING— they get very juicy in the middle and sweet on the outside. Cooking radishes brings out an entirely different side of the vegetable, much mellower than the punchy bite of a raw radish. This is wonderful with standard cherry belles or French breakfast radishes, but it's also a great way to work with mixed bunches of all different colors. Amethyst, a bright purple variety, is especially beautiful roasted. This recipe makes more sauce than you need, but you'll be happy for the extra. Use it as a salad dressing, on other roasted vegetables, or on grilled beef or lamb.

SERVES 4

RADISHES

1½ tablespoons olive oil

3 bunches radishes (about 1½ pounds), greens removed, halved lengthwise

¾ teaspoon kosher salt

SAUCE

6 ounces cubed or crumbled feta

¼ cup olive oil

1 tablespoon fresh lemon juice

1 tablespoon red wine vinegar

½ cup (packed) fresh mint leaves

Freshly ground black pepper

Chicken or vegetable stock or water

1. Preheat the oven to 425°F.

2. Roast the radishes: Pour the oil onto a rimmed baking sheet, tilting the sheet to spread it evenly. Place the radishes in the oil, turning to coat them, and then arrange each radish, cut-side down, on the sheet. Sprinkle with salt. Roast until the radishes are deeply golden on the cut side, 25 to 30 minutes.

3. While the radishes roast, **make the sauce:** Combine the feta, olive oil, lemon juice, vinegar, mint, and several grinds of pepper in a blender. Blend until smooth, adding up to 3 tablespoons stock to make the sauce pourable.

4. To serve, puddle the sauce on a platter or four individual plates. Top with the radishes.

ASPARAGUS AND BACON PASTA

MY DAUGHTER SADIE AND I WENT TO ITALY during the time I was writing this book, and although the trip was all pleasure and no work, I couldn't help but scribble notes down in my little book when a vegetable had been well treated. Sadie ended up doing the same, and often at the end of the day, we'd compare notes, trying to figure out exactly what had made that particular cream sauce or pizza so mind-blowing. We both agreed that this dish needed to be recorded and reproduced.

It was one course of many at a farm restaurant outside of Bologna, and I kept thinking about it in the days after first tasting it. The asparagus/cream/pasta combination is a common spring menu item in Italy, but this particular version was so light, and the tarragon infused it all with a perfume that brought out the best flavors in every element of the dish. Luckily, we came home to my asparagus patch in overdrive, and we all had no qualms with testing this recipe over and over again.

SERVES 4

6 ounces bacon (6 to 8 slices)
1 pound asparagus, sliced on the diagonal into 1-inch pieces
Kosher salt
12 ounces fusilli or other short curly pasta
2 tablespoons unsalted butter
¼ cup finely chopped fresh tarragon
3 tablespoons all-purpose flour
1¼ cups whole milk
½ cup heavy cream
Freshly ground black pepper
2 cups frozen peas (or fresh, if you have them)

1. Preheat the oven to 425°F.

2. Lay the bacon slices on a rimmed baking sheet. Bake until the edges begin to crisp, about 6 minutes. Remove the baking sheet from the oven, and use tongs to turn each slice. Shift the bacon slices close to one another to free up at least a third of the baking sheet.

3. Spread the asparagus pieces on the empty third of the baking sheet, tossing them in the rendered bacon fat. Sprinkle the spears with salt, and return the tray to the oven. Roast until the bacon is very crisp and the asparagus is dark green with slightly wrinkled skin, 7 to 8 minutes. Remove the baking sheet from the oven, and transfer the bacon to a paper-towel-lined plate to drain. Leave the asparagus on the baking sheet.

4. Meanwhile, cook the pasta. Bring a large pot of salted water to a boil, add the pasta, reduce the heat to medium-high, and boil until tender, 11 to 13 minutes. Drain the pasta and return the empty pot to medium heat.

5. Melt the butter in the pot, then add the tarragon. Whisk in the flour and let the mixture cook, whisking once or twice, until it colors and smells nutty, 2 to 3 minutes. Slowly whisk in the milk and cream. Raise the heat to medium-high and bring the mixture to a low boil, whisking as it thickens, 2 to 4 minutes.

Season with salt and pepper. Add the peas, stirring to thaw them (or cook them, if they're fresh) in the sauce. When the peas are warm, remove the pot from the heat.

6. Add the pasta and asparagus to the warm sauce. Crumble the bacon into small bits into the pot, and stir to coat everything in the sauce. Taste and finish with more salt and pepper, if necessary.

BEET AND
BEET GREEN
RISOTTO

ONCE, WHILE I WAS VISITING MY UNCLE during a break from college, he decided I couldn't become an adult without learning how to make risotto. The secret, he claimed, was the magical shallot—part onion, part garlic, all heaven. He instructed me never to fall prey to claims of risotto shortcuts, as the whole point of the dish was to *stir*.

I fall prey to all sorts of things, and I've always felt that if it *can* be easier, it *should* be easier. I've made risotto in the pressure cooker, the slow cooker, and even the oven. But in the end, I think he was right. The texture of the rice never quite seems as good when I've taken a shortcut, and the sauce doesn't get as creamy. And sometimes I make risotto because part of me needs an excuse to stand and stir for a while. Especially in the moments when I don't feel as if I have any time, half an hour of holding that wooden spoon in my hand while I stare out the window seems to be the perfect remedy.

Risotto is a great way to feature so many vegetables. Mushrooms, peas, asparagus—they all seem to find their way into risotto at one time or another. But I love this beet risotto because it uses both the beets and their greens. I like to leave the beets with a bit of crunch, so they lighten up the rice and provide a layer of texture. Treat this as a main dish—it's really got all the elements for a one-bowl dinner—or serve it alongside a roast chicken and greens for a real feast. Don't try to reheat risotto on day two; rather, press it into patties and fry them in a skillet.

SERVES 4 TO 6

1 bunch beets with greens (about 1½ pounds)

5 cups chicken or vegetable stock

Kosher salt

2 tablespoons unsalted butter

1 tablespoon olive oil

½ cup finely chopped shallot (from 2 to 3 ounces shallots)

1½ cups Arborio rice

½ cup white wine (the drier the better) or vermouth

4 ounces chèvre

Zest of 1 lemon

Freshly ground pepper

1. Separate the beets from their greens, and wash both. Peel and finely chop the beets. Chop the greens into thin ribbons, leaving the tough stems behind. Discard the stems or freeze them for future stock.

2. Heat the stock in a medium saucepan set over medium-high heat until it steams. Season with salt to taste. Reduce the heat to low.

3. Melt the butter and olive oil in a large, wide pan or skillet set over medium heat. When the foam from the butter has nearly subsided, add the shallot. Cook, stirring often, until the shallot loses its color, about 3 minutes. Add the beets and cook, stirring often, for about 5 minutes. Add the rice, and continue to stir until it's glossy and bright red from the beets,

2 minutes. Add the wine, and stir until the rice absorbs the liquid, 2 to 3 minutes.

4. Use a ladle to scoop ½ cup of warm stock into the pan, and then stir and stir until the liquid is absorbed into the rice, 2 to 3 minutes. Repeat the process of adding stock, stirring until absorbed, adding more stock, stirring again. After about 10 minutes, add the beet greens, folding them in by the handful to integrate them into the risotto. Continue the pouring and stirring process until you've used almost all of the stock, 10 to 15 minutes more. Taste a grain of rice and a bit of beet. The rice should be tender but not mushy, and the beet should be cooked but with a bit of snap to it. If you're there, remove the pan from the heat. Otherwise, continue with the remaining stock.

5. Stir the chèvre and lemon zest into the risotto. Taste and add more salt, if it needs it. Finish with lots of pepper.

ON USING ROOTS AND THEIR GREENS TOGETHER

"Just take the tops off."

That's the biggest request regarding a bunch of roots at the farmers' market. Sometimes I nod and see there's no room for discussion. There's plenty in the world to argue about, and I don't think vegetables need to be on that list. So I wrap my hands around the stems and twist until the stems break free of the roots. The greens go in a bucket for compost, and the roots go in a bag to go home. Just beets. Just kohlrabi. Just turnips. No greens.

But other times, I see that I might be able to find a home for those greens.

"Have you tried cooking beet greens? You can use them like Swiss chard!"

So often we just do what we've always done, and we don't think of the other options. But the greens of roots are greens like any other. If you're buying beets or turnips, you might as well take those free greens and make use of them. Especially if you're cooking that beet or that turnip, the greens go especially well with their roots. The common flavors of the plant come through when you combine the roots with their greens, and they always complement each other.

If you're buying roots with the greens attached, separate the two when you get home and store them in separate bags. They'll stay fresher that way. Kohlrabi greens are hearty like collards or kale, but beet greens and turnip greens are tender like Swiss chard or spinach, cooking down to silky strips. Radish greens are tasty, too, although they need a little heat and oil to tame the hairy quality they tend to have.

SALTY, SPICY BROCCOLI RAAB PASTA

MY FAVORITE WAY TO COOK BROCCOLI RAAB is to roughly chop an entire bunch, discarding the last inch or two of stem. If there are flowers in the bunch, even better. Put the whole mess of it into a wide saucepan with an inch of water and a knob of butter. Bring it up to a boil, lower the heat, and cover the pan. Cook, stirring occasionally, until the broccoli raab is tender and deep green, 3 to 4 minutes. Toss the raab in the buttery water, drain off any excess liquid, and sprinkle crunchy salt and crushed red pepper flakes over the whole pan. Broccoli raab really needs two things to tame its bitterness and make the leaves tender and silky: a quick boil in water and a whole lot of butter or oil. This accomplishes both, and I can eat a whole bunch this way if there's no one to share it with me.

That being said, my favorite way to feed broccoli raab to *other people* is in this pasta dish. It's so quick and special, and the tangle of leaves and flowers with the half-melted cheese and buttery pasta is a luscious thing to twirl with a fork. Feel free to adjust the spice to your liking. If you can handle more red pepper flakes, go for it.

SERVES 4

Kosher salt

12 ounces spaghetti, linguine, or fettuccine

1 bunch broccoli raab leaves, stems, and flowers (about 1 pound), woody stem ends removed, roughly chopped

2 tablespoons unsalted butter

2 tablespoons olive oil

8 to 10 anchovies in oil, rinsed and finely chopped

1½ tablespoons minced or pressed garlic (4 to 6 cloves)

¼ teaspoon crushed red pepper flakes

½ pound fresh mozzarella, cut or torn into bite-sized pieces

1. Bring a large pot of salted water to a boil. Add the pasta and cook, stirring once or twice, for about 5 minutes. Add the broccoli raab to the pot with the pasta and cook until the pasta is tender, 3 to 4 minutes. Drain the pasta and broccoli raab in a colander and return the pot to medium heat.

2. Place the butter and olive oil in the pot, and heat until the butter melts. Remove the pot from the heat, and quickly add the anchovies, garlic, and red pepper flakes. Stir to combine as they cook in the warm oil. Add the pasta and vegetables to the pot and gently toss to coat in the sauce. Fold in the mozzarella.

WHOLE STEAMED SWEET POTATOES WITH SCALLION WATERCRESS SAUCE

UNTIL THE LAST FEW YEARS, I HAD ALWAYS roasted sweet potatoes—just the way my mother taught me (and how I teach you on page 66). But then the world of sweet potatoes opened up, first via Deborah Madison's idea of steaming them whole and eating them as a main dish with a good sauce (which we'll do here), and then through a particular enlightening breakfast with my friend Heather Braaten, who likes to slice up sweet potatoes and fry them in a skillet for breakfast (we'll do that on page 194).

When you cook sweet potatoes whole, they make such a good and filling main dish. Add a bright-green zingy sauce, and the meal gets even better. This tangy scallion and watercress sauce is also a great salad dressing or dipper for Swiss Chard Rolls (page 213). It uses only scallion greens, which are milder than the punchy whites. Look for hearty bunches of watercress with thick stems, not the delicate hydroponic stuff, which will just disappear in the blender.

These sweet potatoes are also wonderful with the sauce from Eggplant Dengaku (page 156), spicy peanut sauce from Gado Gado (page 224), or Yummy Sauce (page 29).

SERVES 4

2 medium sweet potatoes (about 1½ pounds)

½ cup (packed) coarsely chopped scallion greens (from 1 bunch)

1 cup coarsely chopped watercress stems and leaves (from ½ bunch)

½ cup olive oil

3 tablespoons umeboshi vinegar or rice vinegar

1 teaspoon kosher salt

Ghee (store-bought or homemade, page 190), peanut oil, or coconut oil, for frying

½ cup toasted pecans (see page 136), roughly chopped

1. Cook the sweet potatoes: Separate the levels of your steamer. Fill the lower level with a few inches of water and set the pot over high heat to bring the water to a boil. Tuck your sweet potatoes into the upper level of the steamer pot. (If your sweet potatoes are too large for the steamer, put the sweet potatoes in a large pot and fill the bottom with at least an inch of water.) Steam the sweet potatoes until tender all the way through when pricked with a fork, 30 to 40 minutes, depending on their size. Check the water a few times throughout the cooking process to

(recipe continues)

make sure the pot doesn't dry out. Remove the sweet potatoes from the steamer and cut them in half lengthwise, taking care not to burn yourself as the steam escapes from each sweet potato.

2. Meanwhile, make the sauce: Combine the scallion greens, watercress, olive oil, vinegar, and salt in a blender and blend until smooth.

3. Heat a large skillet set over medium heat. Put just enough ghee in the skillet to lightly cover the bottom. Add as many sweet potato halves as will fit, cut-side down. Cook undisturbed until the flesh becomes golden on the edges, 3 to 4 minutes. Serve 2 halves side by side for small sweet potatoes, or a single half for large ones, smothered in scallion sauce and sprinkled with toasted pecans. Store any leftover sauce in the refrigerator for up to 5 days.

HOMEMADE GHEE

Often used in Indian cooking, ghee has a higher smoke point than butter and a much cleaner taste. Use it for baking, frying, or anywhere you might use butter. I especially love to cook pancakes in ghee.

To make ghee at home, melt 1 pound of unsalted butter in a medium skillet set over low heat. Use a spoon to skim off any foam that gathers on the surface. Let the butter heat undisturbed until it's golden and clear and all the white solids have dropped to the bottom of the pan; this will take somewhere between 20 and 30 minutes. Carefully pour the ghee through a cheesecloth-lined strainer into a jar, catching all the solids in the strainer. (You can use those solids as a seasoning for popcorn—they're delicious.) The ghee will solidify in the jar. You can keep it at room temperature for 1 month or in the refrigerator for up to 3 months. (Makes 2 cups.)

BUTTERNUT SQUASH LASAGNA

BUTTERNUT SQUASH NEEDS OUR HELP. Occasionally you will come across a sweet and delicious curvy squash, velvety and bright and densely textured. But more often it lacks flavor in comparison with the kabocha, sweet dumpling, or pumpkin. The flesh can be watery and the skin hard to contend with. That being said, butternut squash is the most widely available winter squash. In the fall there are mountains of it at any grocery store, and a single squash can create many meals. Cook up a batch of silky Butternut Squash Puree (page 69) and you have the basis for soup like Butternut Red Lentil Dal (page 111) or even dessert (page 254).

This lasagna uses every squash-bolstering trick at once, and it's wonderful special-occasion food. Pasta, cheese, pesto, and—most of all—sage brown butter all make butternut squash sing. Like any lasagna, there are many elements involved, but if you have squash puree and roasted tomatoes in the freezer, it can come together quickly. The star here is really the sage. It infuses the butter between every layer, and then crispy sage leaves decorate the top.

SERVES 8

FILLING

4 cups Butternut Squash Puree (page 69)

2 cups whole-milk ricotta

2 teaspoons freshly grated nutmeg

1 teaspoon kosher salt (if using unsalted ricotta)

2 large eggs

½ teaspoon freshly grated black pepper

KALE PESTO

4 cups stemmed, chopped kale (from about ½ bunch)

2 tablespoons roughly chopped garlic (4 to 5 cloves)

1 tablespoon fresh lemon juice

1 teaspoon kosher salt

⅔ cup olive oil

½ cup grated Parmesan cheese

LASAGNA

8 tablespoons (1 stick) unsalted butter

20 fresh sage leaves

1 pound dried lasagna noodles, partially cooked (if you are using fresh pasta, leave it raw)

1½ cups grated Parmesan cheese

10 whole defrosted roasted tomatoes (see headnote on roasting tomatoes, page 155) or whole canned tomatoes

(recipe continues)

1. Make the filling: Combine the squash puree, ricotta, nutmeg, salt, eggs, and pepper in a large bowl. Stir well.

2. Make the pesto: Combine the kale, garlic, lemon juice, and salt in the bowl of a food processor fitted with the chopping blade. Pulse until you have a uniform mixture. Add the olive oil and Parmesan, and pulse again.

3. Preheat the oven to 375°F.

4. Melt the butter in a small skillet or saucepan set over medium heat. Stir constantly, keeping a close eye on the color of the butter. When the foam subsides and the butter turns slightly brown, 3 to 4 minutes, add the sage leaves. As the sage leaves start to curl, remove the pan from the heat and transfer the leaves to a paper-towel-lined plate.

5. Assemble the lasagna: Spread several spoonfuls of the ricotta filling on the base of a 9 × 13-inch baking dish. Top with a quarter of the noodles, then drizzle the noodles with one-quarter of the sage brown butter. Spread one-quarter of the pesto willy-nilly over the butter. Then layer in one-third of the remaining ricotta mixture and one-quarter of the Parmesan. Repeat this process twice more, then finish with the last of the noodles and the rest of the sage butter. Arrange the tomatoes on top of the noodles. Top with the crispy sage leaves and a final dousing of Parmesan. Cover the dish with aluminum foil.

6. Bake for 30 minutes. Remove the foil and continue to cook until the lasagna bubbles, about 5 minutes more. Let it sit for at least 20 minutes before cutting.

BROCCOLI RAAB AND SWEET POTATO HASH

DARK GREEN, SLIGHTLY BITTER BROCCOLI raab, panfried sweet potatoes and peppers, spicy sausage—it's all here. I add an egg to each bowl, and then we get to call it brunch. Incidentally, this is also a very special-diet-friendly dish. But even if you aren't Paleo or gluten-free, it's very satisfying to eat something so delicious that's all veggies and protein. And, of course, this makes a great light weeknight dinner, too.

SERVES 3 TO 4

5 tablespoons olive oil

1 sweet red bell pepper (8 ounces), seeded and thinly sliced

1 cup thinly sliced onion (1 medium onion)

1 pound sweet potatoes (1 to 2), scrubbed and cut into ½-inch dice

8 ounces cooked chorizo or andouille sausage, cut into ½-inch dice

Kosher salt

1 bunch broccoli raab leaves, stems, and flowers (about 1 pound), woody stem ends removed, roughly chopped

4 large eggs

Freshly ground black pepper

1. Heat 1 tablespoon of the olive oil in a large skillet set over medium-high heat. Add the bell pepper and onion, and cook, stirring often, until the pepper softens and shrinks, about 5 minutes. Add an additional tablespoon of olive oil, then lay the sweet potatoes and sausage in the skillet, arranging them so that as many are touching the bottom of the skillet as possible. Let the sweet potatoes and sausage sit undisturbed for about 5 minutes, then stir, reduce the heat to medium-low, and cover the skillet. Cook, stirring occasionally, until the sweet potatoes are tender and the sausage is brown, 15 to 20 minutes.

2. Meanwhile, cook the broccoli raab. Bring a medium pot of generously salted water to a boil. Add the broccoli raab and cook until the stems are tender, about 2 minutes. Drain in a colander, and toss with 1 tablespoon of the olive oil. Divide the broccoli raab among four bowls.

3. When the sweet potato mixture is ready, sprinkle with ¼ teaspoon salt, and pile it on top of the broccoli raab. Return the skillet to medium heat, and add the remaining 2 tablespoons of olive oil. Crack the eggs into the skillet, sprinkling each one with salt and black pepper. Cover the skillet and cook until the whites of the eggs are cooked but the yolks are runny, 4 to 5 minutes. Use a spatula to slide one egg into each bowl, and drizzle the eggs with any olive oil still left in the skillet.

BRAISED ENDIVES WITH BITTER CARAMEL

I LOVE TO EAT ENDIVE AS IF I WERE taking the petals off a flower. The shape and crunch is so satisfying, and the line between sweet and bitter blurs with each bite. I often use them as a receptacle for dips and salads, as in Chickpea Salad in Endive Boats (page 219), or I eat them plain, snapping my way through each leaf. But a cooked endive takes on an entirely different quality. This dish is really for bitter lovers, as the heat and cream contrive to create a dish that's all juice and heady bitterness. My recipe tester Lissa, who struggles to love some bitter flavors, said she couldn't handle this one. I sent it to Janet, another friend who, like me, craves bitter greens, and she responded with this: "There's all that braising and fat and sweetness and tart lemon! *What bitterness?* It's perfect. I would eat a gallon of this when either sad or happy." To each their own. But, like Janet, I think this is perfect, especially with polenta and roast chicken to merge with all that wonderful sauce.

NOTE For a quicker version with the same flavors, roughly chop the endive. Cook, stirring often in the butter, until wilted, 2 to 3 minutes. Add the sugar and lemon and cook uncovered, continuing to stir, until the endives release juice, 2 to 3 minutes. Add the cream and cook until slightly thickened, 2 minutes.

SERVES 4 TO 6

6 heads of Belgian endive (about 1½ pounds)
3 tablespoons unsalted butter
1 tablespoon sugar
2 tablespoons fresh lemon juice (1 lemon)
2 tablespoons heavy cream
Kosher salt and freshly ground black pepper

1. Remove any bruised leaves from each endive, trim the stem ends, and cut each head in half lengthwise.

2. Melt the butter over medium heat in a large Dutch oven or skillet with a cover. Arrange the endives in the pan, cut-side down—it's okay to crowd them. Let the endives sit undisturbed until the cut side is golden, 4 to 5 minutes. Flip the endives and cook until the underside just begins to color, another 1 to 2 minutes.

3. Reduce the heat to low. Sprinkle the sugar over the endives, add the lemon juice, and cover the pan. Let the endives cook until tender when pricked with a fork, 5 to 7 minutes.

4. Use tongs to transfer the endives to a plate, letting any liquid from the endive remain in the pan. Raise the heat on the pan to medium, and add the cream. Bring the liquid to a low boil, stirring and scraping the bottom of the pan to integrate any brown bits into the sauce as it thickens. Pour the sauce over the endives, and top with a sprinkle of salt and freshly ground pepper.

BRAISED KABOCHA SQUASH WITH MISO AND PURPLE CABBAGE

THE BRIGHT ORANGE FLESH OF KABOCHA squash is creamy and starchy, almost like a perfectly baked potato. Its low water content makes it less ideal for purees, but braised or stewed, it becomes tender, succulent, and almost meaty. There are two kinds of kabocha you might find, and both are great for this recipe. Green kabocha is a bit starchier and earthier, and the bright-orange "red" kabocha is sweeter and a bit creamier. Either way, the skin is thin and delicious, so I tend to roughly peel it, leaving streaks of green or orange on the bright flesh.

Kabocha is a central vegetable in Japanese cuisine, and it pairs especially well with salty miso. This simple dish is so beautiful—all orange and purple—and although there's no meat or other protein, the richness of the squash and hearty cabbage make it as filling and nurturing as any meaty stew. The miso-coconut broth is really good, so you can slurp it plain or serve it over soba noodles or rice. Look for kombu or wakame at an Asian grocer or in the international section of your grocery store. This recipe uses only half a kabocha squash. Put the other half in a freezer bag and freeze it—then pull it out and defrost in the fridge the next time you want to make this recipe (it will be soon!).

SERVES 6

3 cups water

1 6-inch-length kombu or wakame seaweed

1 tablespoon neutral oil, such as grapeseed or sunflower

½ cup roughly chopped onion (½ onion)

1 tablespoon grated fresh ginger

3 cups roughly chopped purple cabbage (from ½ small cabbage)

½ medium kabocha squash, seeded and roughly peeled, cut into thin wedges

½ teaspoon kosher salt

¼ cup white or red miso paste

1 13.6-ounce can full-fat coconut milk

For serving: Chopped scallions (white and light green parts)

(recipe continues)

1. Combine the water and kombu in a bowl. Let the kombu soak for at least 15 minutes.

2. Meanwhile, heat the oil in a wide pot set over medium heat. Add the onion and ginger, and cook, stirring frequently, until soft, 5 to 7 minutes. Add the cabbage and cook, stirring occasionally, until the cabbage begins to wilt, 3 to 4 minutes. Add the kombu soaking water to the pot, holding back the kombu itself. Roughly chop the kombu, and add it to the pot. Add the squash and salt, increase the heat to medium-high, and bring the liquid to a low boil. Cover the pot, reduce the heat to medium-low, and cook until the squash is tender and creamy when pricked with a fork, 12 to 15 minutes. Remove the pot from the heat.

3. Stir together the miso and coconut milk in a small bowl, stirring to thin out the miso and loosen the fat in the coconut milk. Stir the miso mixture into the broth gently to avoid breaking up the squash. If necessary, return the pot to medium until the broth is warmed through. Top with the scallions.

ROASTED VEGETABLE AND CASHEW CURRY

CURRIES CAN HAVE SUCH A TAKEOUT MYStique to them, but they're so easy to make at home. I make this gentle coconut curry with roasted vegetables, which stay firm and slightly caramelize around the edges. If you have a favorite curry powder blend or someone gifts one to you after their travels to some far-flung land, definitely use that in place of the spices here. Feel free to mix it up, too— cubed sweet potatoes, winter squash, and chickpeas are all great additions.

SERVES 4 TO 6

1 large head of cauliflower (about 2 pounds), cored and cut into medium florets

8 ounces carrots (2 large), halved and cut into 1-inch pieces

2 tablespoons olive oil

Kosher salt

2 tablespoons coconut oil

1 cup finely chopped onion (1 onion)

½ teaspoon fennel seeds

1 tablespoon grated fresh ginger

1 teaspoon ground turmeric

½ teaspoon ground cumin

½ teaspoon ground cinnamon

1 13.6-ounce can whole-fat coconut milk

½ cup water

1 to 3 dried red chiles de arbol, to taste

6 whole cardamom pods

½ cup toasted cashews (see page 136)

2 cups chopped spinach

1 tablespoon fresh lime juice (from ½ lime)

Cooked rice or millet, for serving

1. Preheat the oven to 425°F.

2. Combine the cauliflower, carrots, olive oil, and 1 teaspoon of salt in a large bowl, stirring well to coat the vegetables in the oil. Spread them on a rimmed baking sheet and roast until the cauliflower begins to color and the carrots are tender, 20 to 25 minutes.

3. About 10 minutes before the roasted vegetables are ready, melt the coconut oil over medium heat in a large pot. Add the onion and cook, stirring often, until soft and glossy, about 4 minutes. Add the fennel seeds, ginger, turmeric, cumin, and cinnamon, and continue to cook, stirring often, until the onion absorbs the spices and begins to color, another 4 to 5 minutes. Reduce the heat to medium and add the roasted vegetables, coconut milk, water, chiles, and cardamom pods to the pot. Cook, stirring often, until the coconut milk is warmed through and infused with the spices, about 5 minutes. Stir in the cashews and spinach, and cook, stirring occasionally, for 5 minutes. Remove the pot from the heat and stir in ½ teaspoon salt and the lime juice. Spoon into bowls over the rice, taking care to leave the cardamom pods and chiles behind in the pot.

CREAMY CELERIAC SALAD WITH MAPLE PECANS AND LIME

THIS SALAD FIRST CAME TO ME BY WAY OF my friend Molly, a celery lover who was living in Turkey at the time. She sent me a letter about this marvelous new vegetable she had discovered in Istanbul markets, admitting that it *almost* took the place of her beloved celery, which seemed entirely unknown to Turkish people. I had been working at the farmers' market for a while by then, and I was already familiar with celeriac, this knobby, strange root. I always told people how essential it had become to my beef stew and lentil soup, but I had never eaten it raw. This salad is much like a traditional French celeriac rémoulade, and it taught me to love the raw vegetable as well as the cooked. If you have a food processor, you can use it to make quick work of the grating. It will create a rougher grate than the box grater, but the texture works really well here. And don't be afraid of the maple pecans! Candying them in the pan is quick and simple, and I predict you'll start candying nuts for salads and snacks on regular basis.

SERVES 6

1 tablespoon unsalted butter
1 cup pecans
2 tablespoons maple syrup
⅛ teaspoon cayenne
¼ teaspoon large flake salt, such as Maldon
¾ cup plain whole-milk yogurt
Peel of 1 lime, removed with a vegetable peeler and thinly sliced
2 tablespoons fresh lime juice (1 lime)
¾ pound celeriac (about 1 small), peeled (see page 107) and grated
3 tablespoons chopped flat-leaf parsley
¼ teaspoon kosher salt
Freshly ground black pepper

1. Melt the butter in a small skillet set over medium heat. Add the pecans and toast, stirring until fragrant, 2 to 3 minutes. Push the pecans together in the pan and drizzle with the maple syrup. As the syrup sizzles, continue to stir while the syrup loosens and then gets thick, 2 to 3 minutes. Transfer the nuts to a cutting board, sprinkle them with the cayenne and large flake salt, let cool slightly, and roughly chop them.

2. Stir the yogurt, lime peel, and lime juice together in a medium bowl. Add the celeriac, parsley, salt, and several grinds of pepper, stirring gently to combine. Fold in the nuts just before serving, taking care not to crush them.

CAULIFLOWER CHEESE

I THINK CAULIFLOWER AND BROCCOLI ARE often spoken of in the same breath because they have a similar shape. Each comes in a head that separates out into florets that grow off a central stem. Each relies on its likeness to a tree to get itself into the mouths of toddlers everywhere. And, of course, they do belong to the same big family of cruciferous vegetables that also boasts cabbage, kale, kohlrabi, and so many other delicious leafy vegetables. But at the end of this list, they go their separate ways—broccoli snapping and crunching and shining under tamari or lemon, and cauliflower melting with a starchy creaminess that broccoli could never claim. Cauliflower melts into soups and sauces, and it roasts more like a potato, browning and crisping on the outside to protect the creamy flesh of its center.

Cauliflower's high starch content also inspires those in search of pasta and rice alternatives to transform it into "rice" and "pasta." I like to call a vegetable a vegetable (what is there to be ashamed of?), but this classic British dish plays on the ability of the cauliflower to play the part of pasta. It's the most delicious baked mac and cheese, without a mac in sight. Although you might be tempted to serve it as a veggie side, think of it as a main dish. I picked up the tip of infusing the milk from the British food writer Nigel Slater, and that really does make this extra wonderful.

SERVES 4

3 cups whole milk

1 bay leaf

½ small onion, unchopped

2 garlic cloves, halved

Kosher salt

1 large head of cauliflower (about 2 pounds), cut into large uniform florets, stem thinly sliced

4 tablespoons (½ stick) unsalted butter, plus more for greasing the dish

4 tablespoons all-purpose flour

1 teaspoon smoked paprika

1 tablespoon Dijon mustard, or more to taste

Freshly ground black pepper

1 cup grated sharp Cheddar cheese (4 ounces)

½ cup grated Parmesan cheese

¾ cup panko or rough homemade bread crumbs

1 tablespoon olive oil

(recipe continues)

1. Heat the milk in a saucepan set over medium heat. Add the bay leaf, onion, and garlic. Bring the milk to a low boil that bubbles on the surface, then remove the pan from the heat, cover, and let the milk infuse for 15 minutes.

2. Meanwhile, bring a large pot of salted water to a boil. Add the cauliflower and boil until tender, about 4 minutes. Drain the cauliflower in a colander, shaking it to eliminate excess water. Butter an ovenproof 9 × 9-inch or equivalent baking dish, and pack the cauliflower into it.

3. Preheat the oven to 425°F.

4. Melt the butter in a medium saucepan set over medium heat. Whisk in the flour and cook, whisking constantly, until the mixture colors and becomes a nutty-smelling paste, 2 to 3 minutes. Reduce the heat to medium-low. Use a ladle to start adding the hot infused milk to the butter mixture, leaving the bay leaf, onion, and garlic in the pan. Continue adding the milk, whisking to incorporate and prevent the mixture from clumping. When all the milk is in the saucepan, increase the heat to medium-high. Keep cooking and whisking until the mixture comes just to a boil and thickens, 2 to 3 minutes. Remove the pot from the heat and stir in the paprika, mustard, 1 teaspoon salt, and several grinds of pepper. Stir in the grated Cheddar. Taste the sauce, and adjust the salt and mustard, if necessary. Pour the sauce over the cauliflower, top with the Parmesan cheese, bread crumbs, and a drizzle of olive oil.

5. Bake until the sauce bubbles and the bread crumbs are golden, 15 to 20 minutes.

BIG SKILLET CAULIFLOWER PASTA

THIS IS MY FAVORITE KIND OF SKILLET cooking. I roast the cauliflower and sausage right in my big cast-iron skillet in the oven while the pasta and spinach cook together on the stove top. A little pasta water, a little goat cheese, and this all comes together in an incredibly satisfying one-bowl meal. I love the spice andouille brings to this, but you can make it milder by using a sweeter sausage. This dish is also great cold, so leftovers make a stellar lunch. You really need to use a large pan here; anything smaller than a 12-inch skillet just won't cut it. If you don't have a skillet big enough, use a large roasting pan.

SERVES 4, WITH LEFTOVERS

1 large head of cauliflower (about 2 pounds), cored and cut into small florets

6 ounces cooked andouille sausage, quartered lengthwise and sliced ½ inch thick

2 tablespoons olive oil

¾ teaspoon whole cumin seeds

Kosher salt

12 ounces bow-tie pasta or orecchiette

12 ounces spinach, large stems removed, roughly chopped

4 ounces chèvre

Freshly ground black pepper

1. Preheat the oven to 425°F.

2. Spread the cauliflower florets and sausage over the bottom of your largest ovenproof skillet. It's okay if they overlap. Drizzle with the olive oil, and sprinkle with the cumin seeds and ½ teaspoon salt. Roast until the cauliflower is golden, 25 to 30 minutes.

3. Meanwhile, cook the pasta. Bring a large pot of salted water to a boil. Add the pasta and cook until tender, 10 to 12 minutes. Add the spinach during the last 20 seconds of cooking. Scoop out about 1 cup of pasta water, then drain the pasta and spinach in a colander. Do not rinse.

4. Carefully remove the skillet from the oven. Add the pasta and spinach to the skillet with about half the reserved pasta water. Crumble the chèvre (or just gently break it up with your hands, depending on its texture) over the pasta. Gently stir, adding a touch more pasta water to melt the cheese. Season with additional salt, if needed, and lots of pepper.

INDIAN SPICED SHEPHERD'S PIE

WHEN I COME INTO A BOUNTY OF RUTA-
baga, shepherd's pie is the first thing I make.
Rutabaga is the secret ingredient here—it
brings a sweetness and complexity to the topping. It's so good in a mash and especially
wonderful with meat. This version of the old
meat-and-potatoes classic is transformed with
ground lamb, Indian spices, and, of course,
rutabaga.

SERVES 6 TO 8

2 pounds rutabagas (about 2 rutabagas),
peeled, quartered and cut into 1-inch slices

2 pounds red or Yukon Gold potatoes
(5 to 7 potatoes), peeled or unpeeled as
preferred, quartered

4 tablespoons (½ stick) unsalted butter

½ teaspoon cumin seeds

½ teaspoon brown or yellow mustard seeds

¼ teaspoon crushed red pepper flakes

1 pound ground lamb

1 teaspoon ground turmeric

½ teaspoon ground coriander

1½ cups chopped celery (2 to 3 stalks)

2 cups thinly sliced cabbage (from ½ small
cabbage)

1 cup chopped onion (1 onion)

1½ cups chopped peeled carrots
(3 to 4 carrots)

¼ cup water or stock (chicken, beef, or
vegetable)

2 cups fresh or frozen peas

2 teaspoons kosher salt, or more to taste

Freshly ground black pepper

¾ cup whole milk

¼ cup grated Parmesan cheese

½ teaspoon sweet paprika

1. Put the rutabagas into a pot, cover with a bit more than twice their volume in water, and bring to a boil. Reduce the heat to medium-low, cover, and simmer for 10 minutes. Add the potatoes, topping off with additional hot water, if necessary, to make sure that everything is covered. Cook until both roots are tender, 25 to 30 minutes. Drain in a large colander.

2. Meanwhile, melt 2 tablespoons of the butter in a large, shallow ovenproof Dutch oven or skillet set over medium-high heat. Add the cumin seeds, mustard seeds, and red pepper flakes, and cook, stirring constantly, until the seeds pop and color, about 30 seconds. Add the lamb to the pan and cook, stirring often, as the meat releases liquid and then begins to brown, about 10 minutes. Reduce the heat to medium-low and add the turmeric, coriander, celery, cabbage, onion, and carrots. Continue to cook, stirring often, until the vegetables soften, about 10 minutes. Add the water, bring to a boil, cover the pot, and reduce the heat to medium-low. Cook until the vegetables are very tender, another 10 to 12 minutes. Add the peas, 1 teaspoon of the salt, and several grinds of pepper. Cook for another few minutes, stirring to defrost the frozen peas (or cook them, if they're fresh). Taste, and add more salt or pepper if necessary. Remove from the heat.

3. Heat the milk and 1 tablespoon of the butter in a small saucepan over medium heat. Mash the potatoes and rutabagas in a large bowl with a potato masher, adding the hot milk mixture as you go. Add the remaining 1 teaspoon of salt and several grinds of pepper to the mash. Taste and adjust seasonings as necessary.

4. Spread the rutabaga mixture over the stew so that it covers it entirely. Dot with the remaining 1 tablespoon of butter, and then sprinkle the Parmesan cheese and paprika over the top. Put the whole pot under the broiler (at a medium setting, if you have the option), watching carefully, until puffed and golden, 10 to 13 minutes.

CELEBRATIONS
AND OTHER
EXCUSES TO EAT
WITH YOUR HANDS

I BARELY USED A FORK UNTIL I WAS TEN YEARS OLD. I WASN'T RAISED by wolves; rather, I was raised by a single mother who did her best. She fed me noodles and butter and cheesy broccoli (page 51) most nights and didn't focus on the magic of family dinner, mostly making sure I had something to eat and a decent time eating it. It all seems to have worked, as now my culinary tastes have expanded, and I'm fairly adept with a fork and even sometimes a knife.

That being said, eating with my hands still is one of my greatest pleasures. It feels both intimate and celebratory, like a step outside of how we should eat. Even more, those foods that lend themselves to forkless delivery also tend to make good party food. Sad and dried-out supermarket crudités are nothing to get excited about, but slice a pile of gorgeous watermelon radishes and smear them with herb butter, and you'll have hands fighting their way in. People will ask what you did to these radishes, and you'll have to make up something more impressive than just choosing a really beautiful radish and adding salt and butter.

This chapter is full of food for celebrations: platter salads that look like art on the table, big beautiful pan-sized pizzas, and little bits of vegetables to dip in sauce. These recipes can be party food, but they also might just be what you want for an ordinary Thursday night that needs a little fancying up, or a predinner snack for a night that feels a little sparkly. And, of course, there are a few sweets, because what's a celebration (or a book!) without a few good desserts to end the meal.

SWISS CHARD ROLLS

WHENEVER ANYONE I KNOW HAS A BABY, MY friend Janet's post-baby meal is always the one they look forward to the most. My friend Molly talked about *her* meal for ages, most of all about how Janet had created these perfect little Swiss chard rolls. Years later, when I was pulling together recipes for this book, I finally asked Janet what those rolls were. I readied myself for the revelation of the recipe in the hopes that I, too, could make these magical Swiss chard rolls.

Janet squinted her eyes, looking back in time at all the post-baby visits. "Pretty sure I boiled a bunch of Swiss chard, rolled the whole thing into a big log, and sliced it."

Apparently that was enough. Apparently, when you really need the gift of a beautiful meal, rolled Swiss chard tastes a lot better than Swiss chard in a pile. And, of course, it's always more fun to eat with your hands. I played with this a bit, adding a few more elements. The basil and scallions are so nice with the chard, and the cucumbers add the right amount of crunch. Feel free to take this simple base and complicate it. One of my testers tried this same arrangement with soft goat cheese and bacon, and, naturally, it went well, as all things with goat cheese and bacon do. I like this with a simple dipping sauce, but you could also serve with a peanut sauce (see page 224) or scallion watercress sauce (see page 188)—really anything that goes well with greens.

SERVES 4

ROLLS
Kosher salt

2 large bunches Swiss chard, stems trimmed at the base of each leaf

½ cup finely chopped scallions (white and green parts)

½ cup (packed) fresh basil leaves

1 large cucumber, cut into long, thin matchsticks

2 tablespoons toasted sesame seeds (see page 136)

SAUCE
2 tablespoons tamari or soy sauce

2 tablespoons rice vinegar

(recipe continues)

1. Bring a large pot of generously salted water to a boil. Have ready a bowl of ice water nearby.

2. Submerge half the Swiss chard in the boiling water and cook until tender, 3 to 4 minutes. Taste a leaf to make sure it's tender and well salted, giving the other leaves more time or the water more salt if it's needed. Transfer the Swiss chard to the ice water to cool completely. If the water gets warm, add more ice. Repeat with the remaining Swiss chard leaves. Use your hands to wring as much water as possible out of the cooled greens, and unfurl the leaves on the counter. You don't have to be delicate about it, but try to avoid making holes in the leaves.

3. If you've ever rolled maki rolls, the process is similar: Lay out the largest and most intact leaf on the counter, with its stem parallel to the end of the counter, then stack another 5 or 6 leaves on it. Sprinkle a handful of scallions in a line just below the stem, closer to you. Add a row of basil leaves over the scallions, then a row of cucumber sticks. Now grab ahold of the side of that bottom leaf closest to you and patiently but firmly roll the greens over the filling and into a log, tightly rolling away from you. Slice the log into 1-inch slices and arrange them on a plate. Repeat the rolling process with the remaining leaves and filling ingredients. Sprinkle sesame seeds over the top of the sliced rolls.

4. To make the sauce, combine the tamari and rice vinegar in a small bowl. Serve alongside the Swiss chard rolls for dipping.

SCALLION CREPES

MOST RECIPES CALL FOR THE USE OF THE very end of the scallion—that white firm bit just above the root. That's the most oniony part of the scallion, and a handful of thinly slivered white scallions will add a bite and pop to anything. But what about the rest of the scallion? There's an expanse of sweet greens attached to that root, and that's my favorite part of the vegetable. Often this section is more neglected in grocery-store bunches, and you might have to trim and pick away the slimy bits. But if you're getting your scallions from a farmer, you'll often end up with a foot or more of pristine greens, and this is the moment for scallion crepes.

These easy-to-make crepes are a gorgeous bright green, and they provide a good base for so many fillings. Think Chinese scallion pancakes without the kneading or the grease. The high vegetable content makes them slightly more delicate than your average crepe, so be extra gentle when flipping and sliding them out of the pan. To fill them, I go in the blintz direction with ricotta mixed with the white part of the scallion, but they're also great simply brushed with a little Asian sesame oil and tamari. You can also fill them with Hot Sesame Celery with Ruby Cabbage (page 61) for a full-on salty dumpling experience. Save any leftovers in the fridge and reheat them in a frying pan in the morning to eat with a fried egg.

MAKES ABOUT 12 CREPES

CREPES

4 ounces roughly chopped scallion greens (2¼ packed cups, from 2 supermarket bunches or 1 to 2 farmers' market bunches)

1 cup all-purpose flour

½ teaspoon kosher salt

1½ cups whole milk

4 large eggs

3 tablespoons melted unsalted butter, plus more for greasing the pan

FILLING

12 ounces whole-milk ricotta cheese

1 tablespoon fresh lemon juice

2 tablespoons finely chopped scallion whites

Kosher salt

1. Prepare the crepe batter: Combine the scallion greens, flour, salt, milk, eggs, and melted butter in a blender. Blend until as smooth as possible, about 20 seconds in a high-speed blender (such as a Vitamix) and up to 45 seconds in a regular blender. Let sit at room temperature for 30 minutes.

2. Meanwhile, prepare the filling: Stir together the ricotta, lemon juice, and scallions in a medium bowl. Season with salt to taste. Refrigerate until ready to use.

3. When the crepe batter is ready, heat an 8- to 10-inch nonstick skillet or crepe pan over medium heat. Use a cloth or paper towel to grab a bit of butter and carefully run it over the bottom of the pan. Add ¼ cup of the batter to the pan, picking up the pan and swirling it around so the batter covers the whole base of the pan. Let the crepe cook until it forms tiny bubbles, mostly dries out in the center, and releases easily when you move the pan, 1 to 2 minutes. Use a spatula to carefully flip the crepe, or practice your pan-flipping skills, if your wrists are up for it. Cook the second side for 30 seconds, then transfer it to a plate. Repeat with the remaining batter, stacking the crepes as you go.

4. To serve, lay a crepe on the counter and spoon about 1 ½ tablespoons of filling in its center. Fold over two of the sides, and then fold over the other two sides to make a little present. Flip it and lay it on a platter, fold-side down. Repeat with the remaining crepes and filling.

CHICKPEA SALAD IN ENDIVE BOATS

I ALWAYS TRY TO HAVE SOME VARIATION OF this chickpea salad in my fridge. It keeps for days, works great in lunch boxes, and satisfies any craving I have for something fresh and crunchy. It's great on its own or as a side dish for a picnic or potluck. To make it especially pretty, I love to scoop it into endive leaves for a quick and beautiful lunch. Feel free to vary the vegetables according to what you have in your fridge or garden. And if you don't love the bitterness of endive, use butter lettuce leaves instead.

SERVES 6 TO 8

3 tablespoons fresh lemon juice (1 lemon)

3 tablespoons rice vinegar

3 tablespoons extra-virgin olive oil

Kosher salt

½ teaspoon finely minced garlic (1 clove)

⅓ cup finely chopped red onion

3 ounces feta cheese, crumbled or cubed

2 cups cooked chickpeas or 1 15-ounce can, drained

8 ounces cucumbers (2 small Persian or 1 regular cucumber), chopped

1 small fennel bulb, stemmed, quartered lengthwise, and thinly sliced crosswise

⅔ cup chopped radishes (3 to 5 radishes)

⅓ cup roughly chopped flat-leaf parsley

Freshly ground black pepper

2 to 3 endives, leaves separated

1. Whisk together the lemon juice, vinegar, olive oil, and ½ teaspoon salt in a large bowl. Add the garlic, red onion, and feta, gently tossing to coat them in the dressing. Let it all marinate at room temperature for 10 minutes.

2. Add the chickpeas, cucumbers, fennel, radishes, parsley, and several grinds of pepper. Gently fold the ingredients into the dressing. Taste and adjust for salt and pepper, if needed. Transfer to a platter or wide, shallow bowl.

3. Lay out the endive leaves like rays of the sun around the salad. Use the endive leaves to scoop up the salad, or serve each person a scoop of salad and a few endive leaves.

RADICCHIO PIZZA

WHEN OUR GIRLS WERE LITTLE, JOEY AND I made a promise. We told them both that when they turned thirteen, they'd get a trip with me to any place of their choosing. We called it the Thirteen Trip. It seemed like a dream and a milestone for a distant future.

But, of course, it wasn't so distant. Before I knew it, Sadie was getting Lonely Planet guides out of the library. She'd ask for reports from friends returning from vacation, and she kept a running tally in her head of all the places she'd ever dreamed of visiting. In the end, Italy won. And that's how I found myself at a table on a tiny cobblestone street in Rome, learning how good radicchio really can be.

We shared a plate between us that night, a piece of grilled salty Scamorza cheese topped with grilled radicchio, tart cherry tomatoes, and a few paper-thin slices of prosciutto. When radicchio is cooked at a high heat, it loses its gorgeous color, but it gains a deep sweetness, almost as if it were a fire-roasted flower. That radicchio with the salt of the prosciutto and cheese and the tart sugar of the tomatoes was my favorite food combination in Italy, and as I tried to re-create it at home, pizza became the most appropriate vessel. This thick-crust pizza is cooked in a sheet pan, and all the toppings piled on in a messy and gorgeous way that requires napkins and a sense of humor. If you don't have time in your day to make the dough, you can absolutely create this on a few store-bought crusts.

MAKES ONE 18 × 13-INCH PIZZA

DOUGH
1¼ cups warm water

1 teaspoon sugar

2 teaspoons active dry yeast

3 cups all-purpose flour, plus more for the work surface

⅓ cup rye, spelt, or whole-wheat flour

1 teaspoon kosher salt

2 teaspoons olive oil, plus more for greasing the bowl

PIZZA
¼ cup plus 2 tablespoons olive oil, plus more for drizzling

1 tablespoon minced garlic (from 4 to 6 cloves)

¾ pound fresh mozzarella, thinly sliced

1 pint (10 to 12 ounces) cherry tomatoes, halved

1 medium head of radicchio (10 to 12 ounces), cored and sliced into thin strips

Kosher salt

3 ounces thinly sliced prosciutto

2 tablespoons balsamic vinegar

1. Make the dough: Combine the warm water and sugar in a liquid measuring cup, stirring to dissolve the sugar. Sprinkle the yeast over the surface of the water and let stand for 10 minutes.

2. Combine the flours, salt, and the 2 teaspoons oil in the bowl of a food processor. Pulse to combine. With the machine running, add the yeast mixture as fast as the flours will absorb it. Process until the dough forms a ball and clings to the blade, about 30 seconds, then process for another 30 seconds. Place the dough in a large, greased bowl, cover it with plastic wrap or a clean dish towel, and leave in a warm place to rise. You can use the dough in 2 to 3 hours, but, if possible, leave it for 6 to 8 hours, as the flavor will be tangier and more developed. I like to make the dough in the morning for that night's dinner.

3. Make the pizza: About 2 hours before you're ready to eat, turn the dough out on a lightly floured counter. Press it into a rough rectangle, and let it rest for 15 minutes. Meanwhile, pour the ¼ cup olive oil onto a rimmed half sheet pan (18 × 13 inches). Move it around to spread the olive oil over the entire base of the pan.

4. Use a rolling pin to roll the dough into a large rectangle nearly large enough to fit in the sheet pan. Carefully transfer the dough to the pan, and pat and pull the edges to reach the corners. It's okay if they don't quite get there, just do your best. Cover the sheet pan with plastic wrap, and leave it in a warm spot until the dough is slightly puffy, 45 minutes to 1 hour.

5. Preheat the oven to 425°F.

6. Combine the remaining 2 tablespoons of olive oil with the garlic in a small bowl. Use a pastry brush to paint the dough with the oil mixture. Alternatively, you can spoon it evenly over the dough. Top with the mozzarella, leaving about 1½ inches free around the perimeter. Bake until the cheese melts and the dough begins to color, about 20 minutes. Remove the pan from the oven.

7. Spread about three-quarters of the tomatoes over the melted cheese, and top with the radicchio. Sprinkle lightly with salt, drizzle with olive oil, and return the pizza to the oven. Bake until the radicchio is entirely wilted and the crust is golden, another 15 to 20 minutes. Remove the pan from the oven. Top the hot pizza with the remaining tomatoes, the prosciutto, and the balsamic vinegar. Let the pizza cool slightly before cutting and serving.

GADO GADO

I'M A FIRM BELIEVER IN THE BRILLIANCE of the platter salad—that is, a combination of every vegetable you want to eat, cooked or uncooked, arranged on a platter for everyone to admire and devour. Some people call it a *composed* salad, but that is far too buttoned up for something I will definitely end up eating with my hands. Gado gado is an Indonesian dish, singular for its inclusion of mostly cooked vegetables, protein from eggs and tofu, and a fantastic peanut sauce to slather over all of it. I use it often as a dinner-party meal for vegetarians, and it's also great for kids with particular tastes, as they can take what they like and leave the rest. Traditionally, the vegetables include potatoes, cabbage, and string beans, but I always tailor it to what I have in the refrigerator. Roasted sweet potatoes or winter squash, fresh snap peas, Hakurei turnips, or carrots would all be at home on the plate here as well. The sauce tastes better the second day, so feel free to make it ahead of time.

SERVES 4 TO 6

PEANUT SAUCE

½ cup peanut butter (smooth or crunchy)

2 medium garlic cloves, sliced

2 tablespoons tamari or soy sauce

2 tablespoons Asian sesame oil

3 tablespoons rice vinegar

1 tablespoon sugar

1 tablespoon sriracha, or more to taste

1 inch unpeeled fresh ginger, sliced

2 tablespoons fresh lime juice (1 lime)

½ cup water

SALAD

1 pound small red or Yukon Gold potatoes (3 to 5 potatoes)

Kosher salt

8 ounces green beans (any color)

4 ounces asparagus, woody ends snipped off

4 cups roughly chopped green cabbage (from ½ head)

4 large eggs

2 tablespoons grapeseed, sunflower, or other neutral oil

1 14-ounce package firm or extra-firm tofu, cubed or cut into 2-inch rectangular lengths

1 teaspoon tamari or soy sauce

1 bunch radishes, greens removed, quartered

2 cups bean sprouts, micro greens, or any other hearty sprout

1 medium cucumber, quartered and cut into 1-inch pieces

Lime wedges, for serving

(recipe continues)

1. Make the peanut sauce: Combine the peanut butter, garlic, tamari, sesame oil, vinegar, sugar, sriracha, ginger, lime juice, and water in a blender. Blend until smooth. Taste and add more sriracha, if needed. Transfer the sauce to a bowl.

2. Prepare the salad ingredients: Put the potatoes in a medium pot and cover them with at least 2 inches of water. Cover the pot and bring the water to a boil over medium-high heat. Cook until the potatoes are tender, 15 to 20 minutes, depending on their size. Drain and let the potatoes cool for a few minutes. Slice them into thick rounds.

3. Meanwhile, bring a second medium pot of generously salted water to a boil over medium-high heat. Add the beans and asparagus to the water, and cook until just tender, about 2 minutes. Use tongs or a skimmer to transfer the beans and asparagus to a colander. Add the cabbage to the water and cook until tender, 3 to 4 minutes. Scoop the cabbage out of the water and let it drain. Finally, add the eggs to the water and cook for 8 minutes. Drain the eggs and run them under cold water. Peel them, and thinly slice or cut each egg in half, depending on your preference.

4. While the vegetables cook, heat the oil in a skillet set over medium-high heat. Add the tofu and cook, stirring often, until browned, 7 to 9 minutes. Add the tamari and continue to cook, stirring often, until the tofu absorbs the tamari and crisps up, 2 to 3 minutes. Remove the pan from the heat.

5. Arrange the cooked vegetables, eggs, tofu, radishes, bean sprouts, cucumber, and lime wedges on a large platter. Serve with the sauce on the side, and let each diner arrange his or her own bowl.

GREEN BEAN TEMPURA NESTS

AT THE JAPANESE RESTAURANT ON MAIN Street in the town where I grew up, you could get a web of thin matchstick-sized vegetables all deep-fried together. It was a beautiful jumble on the plate that was so fun to tackle, and diners would tear off sections and drench them in dipping sauce. Years later, my husband and I discovered how to make them by accident. We were hurrying through a batch of green bean tempura, dipping and frying too many beans at once. The result was a perfect nest, so similar to the one I had eaten as a child.

Yellow wax beans are so good as tempura—especially the skinny ones, which lend themselves to a perfect crispy crunch. Thin green or purple beans are great here, too, or even a mix of whatever you have. Whichever beans you choose, this is a good recipe for thin, fresh, in-season beans. And if you have access to daikon, grate a bit and stir it into the dipping sauce. Daikon helps your body process the grease, and it adds a good spice to the sauce, too. Although Sprite might seem out of place here, pick up a bottle for the recipe. A friend of mine who worked the fry station at Nobu shared this secret with me, and I've never gone back to plain old seltzer. This method also works well with matchsticks of sweet potato or carrot. And while you have the batter, broccoli, onions, scallions, and thinly sliced zucchini can also be used for tempura. Making the batter and dipping sauce while the oil heats is a time-saver, but if you're new to deep-frying and want to keep a close eye on the oil, feel free to make the batter and dipping sauce before you heat the oil.

MAKES 10 TO 12 NESTS

TEMPURA
Corn or vegetable oil, for frying
1¼ cups all-purpose flour
1½ cups Sprite or plain seltzer
1 teaspoon kosher salt, plus more for sprinkling
1 pound thin wax beans, haricot verts, or any thin tender bean, stem ends trimmed

DIPPING SAUCE
3 tablespoons tamari or soy sauce
1 cup water
1 tablespoon sugar
Optional: 2 tablespoons grated fresh daikon, 1 teaspoon grated fresh ginger

1. Fill a large, heavy-bottomed pot with 2 to 3 inches of oil. Set the pot over medium-high heat, cover it, and heat the oil until it registers between 350°F and 375°F on an instant-read thermometer.

2. Meanwhile, whisk together the flour, Sprite, and salt in a wide bowl, doing your best to create a fairly lump-free batter.

3. Make the dipping sauce: Combine the tamari, water, and sugar in a small saucepan set over medium heat. Bring just to a boil, cover the pan, and reduce the heat to low to keep the sauce warm.

(recipe continues)

4. When the oil comes up to temperature, grab a handful of beans and drop them into the batter. Use tongs to grab the beans all at once, shaking off any excess batter. Carefully slide the bunch into the hot oil and let it cook until the batter is golden, about 2 minutes. Flip the bunch and cook for 1 minute, taking care not to let it get too dark. Check the temperature of the oil, and increase the heat if it's cooled a bit. Use a slotted spoon or skimmer to transfer the bunch to a paper-towel-lined plate and sprinkle with salt. Repeat with the remaining beans, making 8 to 10 nests in all. You can cook up to 3 nests at a time, depending on the width of the pot. Just be careful not to pack them in too tightly. And if the nests stick to the bottom of the pot, try to gently release them with a slotted spoon. Add a bit more oil for the next batch and bring it back up to temperature.

5. Serve the nests with the dipping sauce and a little mountain of grated daikon and ginger on the side, if desired. Stir the daikon and ginger into the warm dipping sauce just before eating.

DEEP-FRYING

There's a reason why fried food is so popular at restaurants, and not so popular for home cooks. Deep-frying is one of those cooking methods that is fun to let others do for us, especially when they have a real deep-fryer at their disposal. They can handle the grease facials, the forearm burns, and the challenging task of disposing of all that oil when the night is done. Why would we ever want to do that at home?

You might not, and I give you a full pass. But if you are a bit more intrepid, enjoy a cooking adventure now and then, and have a decent hood over your stove, I think you should go for it. Because when it comes to vegetables, deep-frying is a really great way to cook them. Not all the time, of course! But there's nothing like a tempura night when all the wax beans, zucchini, and scallions are in full force. We open all the doors, face the fans away from the kitchen, and invite friends over for beer and tempura. It's a hands-on, messy kind of party, but it always goes well. And the vegetables never actually make it to the table—they're always eaten just as soon as they won't burn your mouth. If I've convinced you to give it a try, here are a few things to keep in mind:

1. I like deep-frying in a cast-iron Dutch oven. The insulated nature of cast iron helps keep the temperature of the oil, which should hover between 350°F and 375°F, constant. You'll also need an analog or instant-read thermometer to help you monitor the temperature of the oil.

2. You'll need a lot of oil, and this is the moment to go for those big vats of corn or vegetable oil from the bottom shelf of the grocery store. We deep-fry maybe a few times a year, so I don't get too hung up on quality or health benefits (or not) of my chosen oil.

3. Don't ever throw food into the hot oil. Gently lower it in with tongs or a slotted spoon to minimize splashing.

4. When you're finished cooking, remove the oil from heat and let it cool entirely. This will take hours, and sometimes I just let it sit overnight. Then you have a few options. If you've only been cooking vegetables and you want to be thrifty, you can strain the oil back into a clean bottle and use it one more time. The cleaner the oil, the better the taste of the food, but you can absolutely use oil again if it hasn't cooked meat or fish. You can also simply pour it back into a container and throw it away. Or if you know someone who has a car that runs on vegetable oil, strain out the crunchy bits and offer it to them. Just do not pour the oil down the drain, and do not pour it on the ground.

And that's it! The best part is that when you invite other people over to deep-fry in your kitchen, it gives them the confidence to try it on their own. So the next time, they'll be inviting *you* to a tempura party.

SCARLET TURNIP GALETTES

SCARLET TURNIPS ARE MUCH HEARTIER than silky white turnips, with a raw texture closer to a tender beet. They are also much earthier and can stand up to stronger flavors than their white cousins. Put a white turnip in with too many other ingredients or cook it too long, and it will just disappear; the reds, however, will hold up to spice, acid, or herbs. The greens are quite different, too. White turnip greens tend to be spindly and delicate, almost like a radish leaf without the pesky hairiness. But scarlet turnip greens are thick and hearty, closer to kale or kohlrabi.

I never let a fall season go by without making at least one batch of scarlet turnip galettes. The turnips bake up so well in the crust, and the deep purple of the outer skin is a stunner. You can make these with plain goat cheese or use an herbed cheese with garlic or thyme for even more deliciousness in each tart.

MAKES FIVE 5- TO 6-INCH GALETTES

CRUST

1½ cups all-purpose flour, plus more for rolling

¾ cup spelt or whole-wheat pastry flour

1 cup (2 sticks) cold unsalted butter, cut into small pieces

1 tablespoon fresh thyme leaves or 1 teaspoon dried

⅓ cup cold water

2 teaspoons apple cider vinegar

½ teaspoon kosher salt

FILLING

Olive oil

1 bunch scarlet turnips (about 1½ pounds), greens and stems removed, sliced ⅛-inch-thick

1 teaspoon fresh thyme leaves or ½ teaspoon dried

8 ounces chèvre

Large flake sea salt, such as Maldon

1. Make the crust: Combine the flours, butter, and thyme in the bowl of a stand mixer, using your hands to coat the butter in the flours. Put the bowl in the refrigerator. Combine the water, vinegar, and the salt in a measuring cup, stirring to dissolve the salt. Put the vinegar mixture in the freezer for 10 minutes.

2. Remove the bowl and cup from the refrigerator and freezer. Using the paddle attachment, blend the flour mixture on low speed until it has the texture of crumbly meal. With the mixer still running, slowly pour in the vinegar mixture. The dough will be crumbly at first, then after 10 or 20 seconds, it will come together in a ball.

3. Turn the dough out onto the counter. Separate it out in 5 roughly equal pieces weighing about 4 ounces each. Press each section into a disk and wrap in plastic or wax paper. Refrigerate for at least 30 minutes and up to 3 days.

4. Preheat the oven to 400°F. Line two baking sheets with parchment paper.

5. Make the galettes: Generously flour your counter. Roll out one section of dough into a rough circle about 8 inches in diameter. (It can be really rough; any odd edges are fine.) Transfer the circle to the prepared baking sheet, and repeat with a second section of dough. Add that circle to the baking sheet as well, so you have 2 circles of dough ready to go. You'll eventually have 3 galettes on each tray, but you'll need to fill and fold 2 before you'll have room for a third.

6. Pour a bit of olive oil in a small bowl, and use a pastry brush or paper towel to paint each dough circle with it. Arrange the turnip slices on the dough circles in an overlapping circular pattern, leaving about an inch empty along the perimeter of each circle. Add a sprinkle of thyme to each galette, then dot generously with bits of chèvre. Fold the edges of the crust over the filling. Paint the crust with olive oil, drizzle a bit of oil over the turnips, and sprinkle both the filling and the crust with the large flake salt. Shift the galettes closer to each other to make room for a third one on the tray, and repeat the assembly process with a third section of dough. Repeat with the remaining pieces of dough on the other prepared baking sheet.

7. Bake until golden, 35 to 40 minutes. Cool slightly before serving.

WATERMELON RADISHES WITH HERB BUTTER

THERE ARE SOME VEGETABLES THAT ARE so beautiful we eat them with our eyes as much as our mouths. Take carrots, for example. Most are orange, delicious, and beautiful enough. But put an ordinary carrot next to the variety called Purple Haze, and you'll see cousins, one bright orange and the other with an inner circle the color of an eggplant. What's the difference in taste? In a blind taste test, not much. But take a look at what you're eating, and the purple carrot wins. Any vegetable that looks like it's been touched with a watercolor set has the beauty advantage. And this is why salted watermelon radishes with butter are one of my very favorite party foods.

Watermelon radishes tend to make their appearance in the mid- to late summer. They're larger than the classic Cherry Belles, and they can range in size from an inch in diameter to as many as 4 or 5. They are deceptively plain on the outside, smooth as an egg, with a pale white skin that is both pink and green tinged at the same time. Slice through its middle, and you see the watermelon. The center holds a perfect circle of bright pink, surrounded by an outer layer of lime green. It is the most impressive vegetable I know, and it needs very little to make it party ready. They also store well in the refrigerator, so I stock up in the fall, and they stay crisp and ready through New Year's and beyond.

Radishes and butter is a time-honored pair, and this is a great way to present it. Use any compound butter, but some of my favorites here are thyme, tarragon, and chives.

SERVES 6

4 ounces soft Compound Butter (page 32)
1 pound watermelon radishes (4 to 6 radishes), sliced between ⅛ and ¼ inch thick
Large flake sea salt, such as Maldon

Scoop the butter into a small dish or ramekin, and place it in the center of a large platter. Lay the radish slices out in a single layer around the butter. Sprinkle generously with salt. Let the tray sit for at least 10 minutes before serving.

CAULIFLOWER HOT WINGS WITH BLUE CHEESE DRESSING

I FIRST MET THIS RECIPE AT A PARTY THAT sticks in my memory mostly because of the good company and the sparkly night, but also because of one particular dish on the potluck table. It was a mostly gluten-free, local bourbon type of crowd (as tends to happen in my neck of the woods), and this dish was the hum and belle of the party.

Is that harissa? I swear that's adobo. Is this an Ottolenghi recipe? The cauliflower was a hit. In fact, every plate had a generous pile of the spicy red cauliflower—a rapidly disappearing pile, as the correct verb for how the collective party was eating this dish could only be *shoveling*.

There was a chorus of requests for the recipe from around the table. One guy in the corner piped up.

"Good, right? It's Hot Wing Cauliflower. I found it on the Internet."

There was a collective pause as he continued.

"Pretty classic. Dip in flour, coat with hot sauce, that sort of thing."

"But it must be chickpea flour?" someone asked mid bite. "Or rice?"

"I dunno. White? And Frank's hot sauce?"

It really was hot-wing cauliflower. And it set me onto the path of this recipe, for which I am deeply grateful. Use your favorite hot sauce of any spicy level. Frank's RedHot is a great one for this recipe, or something more fancy and fermented is delicious, too. Just keep in mind that the flavor of the hot sauce will be dominant, so choose your spice level mindfully.

SERVES 4

DRESSING
¼ cup mayonnaise
¼ cup plain whole-milk yogurt
¼ cup sour cream
½ tablespoon fresh lemon juice
1 teaspoon rice vinegar
¼ cup crumbled blue cheese
¼ teaspoon minced garlic
Kosher salt and freshly ground black pepper

CAULIFLOWER
1½ cups water
1 cup all-purpose flour
2 teaspoons garlic powder
4 teaspoons smoked paprika
¾ teaspoon kosher salt, plus more for sprinkling
Neutral high-heat oil, such as grapeseed
1 medium head of cauliflower (about 2 pounds), cored, cut into bite-sized pieces, and dried
2 tablespoons unsalted butter
¼ cup hot sauce

1. Make the dressing: Whisk together the mayonnaise, yogurt, sour cream, lemon juice, rice vinegar, blue cheese, and garlic in a small bowl. Add salt and pepper to taste. Refrigerate until ready to serve.

2. Make the batter: Whisk together the water, flour, garlic powder, paprika, and salt in a medium bowl.

3. Heat a large skillet over medium-high heat. (You'll be frying the cauliflower in batches, so you can also get a second skillet going simultaneously if you like.) Pour enough oil into the skillet so it's ¼ inch deep. After a few minutes, test the oil with a drop of water— when it sizzles, it's ready.

4. Submerge several florets in the batter, then transfer them one at a time to the hot oil. Don't pack the skillet. Fry the cauliflower, turning it a few times with a fork, until brown and crispy on all sides, 8 to 10 minutes. Transfer the cauliflower to a paper-towel-lined plate and sprinkle with salt. Repeat with the remaining cauliflower. Transfer the cauliflower to a large, wide bowl or platter.

5. Meanwhile, combine the butter and hot sauce in a small saucepan over medium heat. Cook, stirring often, until the butter melts, 1 to 2 minutes. Pour the hot sauce mixture over the cauliflower, gently folding to coat the cauliflower in the sauce.

6. Serve the cauliflower hot, with the blue cheese dressing for dipping.

THREE PARTY TOASTS

VEGETABLES ON TOAST IS ONE OF THOSE marvelous inventions that is equally appropriate for fancy parties (Parmesan thrown hither and thither on the platter just so, greens piled on sliced artisanal baguette) and haphazard oh-man-I-should-eat-something lunches (last night's zucchini scooped on the bread end no one wanted for toast that morning). Really, both situations are equally delicious, and I look for every opportunity to pile *something* on toast. These three recipes are all geared for party eating, but I give you full permission to scale them down to solo haphazard lunch prep.

BROCCOLI RAAB AND CHEDDAR TOASTS

This is a hopped-up and very green open-faced grilled cheese.

MAKES 6 TO 10 TOASTS

1 bunch broccoli raab leaves, stems, and flowers (about 1 pound), woody stem ends removed, roughly chopped

1 cup water

2 tablespoons olive oil

¼ teaspoon crushed red pepper flakes

¼ teaspoon kosher salt

¼ teaspoon minced garlic (1 small clove)

8 to 10 slices baguette or 6 to 8 slices ciabatta or country-style bread, sliced ½ inch thick

6 ounces sharp Cheddar cheese, thinly sliced or grated

Large flake sea salt, such as Maldon

Freshly ground black pepper

1. Combine the broccoli raab and water in a large sauté pan or saucepan set over medium-high heat. Cover the pan and cook, tossing once or twice to submerge the vegetables in the water, until the stems of the broccoli raab are tender, 5 to 7 minutes.

2. Preheat the broiler to 450°F or medium-high, depending on your broiler options.

3. Tilt the pan into the sink, hold the greens back with a large spoon, and drain off as much water as possible. Alternatively, you can drain the greens in a colander and return them to the pan. Return the pan to medium-high heat, and shuffle the broccoli raab over to one side of the pan. Pour the olive oil into the empty part of the pan and heat until it shimmers, about 45 seconds. Add the red pepper flakes and kosher salt to the olive oil, and let the flakes toast and infuse the oil for a moment. Then stir the broccoli raab into the oil and continue to cook, stirring frequently, for 2 to 3 minutes. Stir in the garlic, and remove the pan from the heat.

4. Lay the bread out on a baking sheet and toast under the broiler until the bread begins to color, 1 to 3 minutes (depending on the heat of your broiler). Flip the bread and toast until the other side is colored, about 30 seconds.

5. Remove the baking sheet from the oven and top the bread with half the Cheddar. Toast just until the cheese melts, about 1 minute. Then remove the sheet from the oven and pile the broccoli raab on each toast, dividing the greens evenly among them. Top each toast with a pinch of the large flake salt and a few grinds of pepper, then add a final layer of Cheddar. Return the toasts to the oven and toast until the cheese melts, 1 more minute.

MELTED ZUCCHINI

This is one of my favorite ways to cook zucchini. It all melts into itself and becomes almost spreadable. This topping is also fantastic on pasta (of course).

MAKES 6 TO 10 TOASTS

2 tablespoons olive oil, plus more for brushing the bread

1½ pounds zucchini, yellow summer squash, or a mix, sliced into paper-thin rounds with a mandoline

½ teaspoon kosher salt

1 small garlic clove, pressed into a paste with a garlic press or the side of a knife

1 teaspoon finely chopped fresh rosemary

⅓ cup grated Parmesan cheese

Freshly ground black pepper

8 to 10 slices baguette or 6 to 8 slices ciabatta or country-style bread, sliced ½ inch thick

1. Preheat the broiler to 450°F or medium-high, depending on your broiler options.

2. Heat the olive oil in a large skillet or saucepan set over medium-high heat. Add the zucchini, a few handfuls at a time, sprinkling it with the salt as you go. Shuffle the zucchini with a spatula to give it contact with the hot pan, then add more, repeating until all the squash is in the pan. Continue to cook, stirring often, until the zucchini melts together and begins to color, 8 to 10 minutes. If it begins to burn or stick on the bottom of the pan, reduce

(recipe continues)

the heat to medium. When the zucchini is melted together in a soft, nearly spreadable mess, take it off the heat. Stir in the garlic, rosemary, cheese, and lots of pepper.

3. Meanwhile, lay the bread on a baking sheet and use a pastry brush to lightly paint the tops of each toast with olive oil. Toast under the broiler until the bread begins to color, 1 to 3 minutes (depending on the heat of your broiler). Flip the bread and toast until the second side is colored, 30 seconds. Transfer the toasts to a serving plate, olive-oil-side up.

4. Spoon the zucchini mixture onto the toasts.

ESCAROLE AND PRESERVED LEMON RICOTTA

Escarole is something between a lettuce and a cooking green, and it works well as either. Raw, it's a hearty lettuce with a texture like romaine, and it makes a great winter salad with apples and Cheddar. I love to braise escarole with butter and water (similar to Butter-Braised Cabbage, page 62), and those wilted greens are the center of this toast. Though bitter when raw, escarole tastes remarkably like the heart of an artichoke when cooked. If you don't have preserved lemon, just grate a bit of lemon zest into your ricotta.

MAKES 6 TO 10 TOASTS

1 large head escarole, roughly chopped

1 tablespoon water

2 tablespoons unsalted butter

Kosher salt

8 to 10 slices baguette or 6 to 8 slices ciabatta or country-style bread, sliced ½ inch thick

Olive oil

8 ounces whole-milk ricotta

Rind of 1 preserved lemon (see page 57), rinsed and finely chopped

Fruity extra-virgin olive oil

1. Preheat the broiler to 450°F or medium-high, depending on your broiler options.

2. Combine the escarole, water, and butter in a large sauté or saucepan set over medium-high heat. Cover the pan and cook, stirring frequently, until the escarole goes limp and bright green, 2 to 3 minutes. Uncover the pan and continue to cook, stirring frequently, until most of the liquid evaporates, 1 more minute. Remove the pan from the heat and lightly sprinkle the greens with salt.

3. Lay the bread on a baking sheet and use a pastry brush to lightly paint the tops of each toast with olive oil. Toast under the broiler until the bread begins to color, 1 to 3 minutes (depending on the heat of your broiler). Flip the bread and toast until the second side is colored, 30 seconds. Transfer the toasts to a serving plate, olive-oil-side up.

4. Stir together the ricotta and preserved lemon rind. Spoon the ricotta onto each toast, dividing it evenly among them. Top with the escarole, a sprinkling of salt, and a light drizzle of fruity extra-virgin olive oil.

SWEET POTATO LATKES WITH ROASTED APPLESAUCE

MY CHILDHOOD HANUKKAH MEMORIES are of the scratch-and-sniff variety, intertwined with the smell of oil in my hair and my clothes that sticks around for days. My grandparents used to invite the whole world over for a party in December, and my grandfather would never leave the stove. I loved the holiday feeling of it all, but I always left feeling ill from the oil that seemed as tenacious as the biblical oil it represented.

These days I don't wait until Hanukkah to make latkes. And I've come to love making them with sweet potatoes, so they're a departure from the classic. Even further, I only fry them for a moment. Most of the cooking happens in the oven, so there's no need to take a shower and open all the windows after I cook. Since the oven is already on, I use it to make applesauce. Roasted applesauce is so easy and wonderful, and I find roasting concentrates the apple flavor while boiling them can really dilute it. Feel free to double or triple the applesauce recipe, as it freezes really well. If you have a food mill, there's no need to even core or peel the apples.

MAKES ABOUT 20 LATKES AND 3 CUPS OF APPLESAUCE

ROASTED APPLESAUCE

4 pounds crisp apples, such as Galas or Pink Ladies, cut into large chunks

2 tablespoons fresh lemon juice (1 lemon)

3 tablespoons maple syrup

2 tablespoons unsalted butter, cut into small pieces

LATKES

1 cup halved and thinly sliced leeks (from 1 leek, using all the white and the tender part of the green)

2 pounds sweet potatoes (2 to 4), peeled and grated

2 large eggs

½ cup matzo meal

2 tablespoons finely chopped fresh sage or 1 teaspoon dried

1 teaspoon kosher salt

½ teaspoon freshly ground black pepper

Neutral oil, such as grapeseed or sunflower

For serving: Sour cream or Greek yogurt

1. Preheat the oven with a rack in the center to 425°F.

2. Start the applesauce: Pile the apples into a large baking dish. Drizzle with the lemon juice and maple syrup, and spread the bits of butter over the apples. Roast until the apples are soft, 30 to 40 minutes. Remove the pan from the oven, and reduce the oven temperature to 350°F.

3. Meanwhile, make the latkes: Combine the leeks, sweet potatoes, eggs, matzo meal, sage, salt, and pepper in a large bowl. Massage the mixture with your hands to combine thoroughly, breaking up the egg yolks as you do.

4. Heat a large skillet over medium-high heat, and add enough oil to cover the bottom of the pan. (If you have a second skillet, you can use that as well and have two pans frying at once.) Keep two ungreased baking sheets nearby. Heat the oil until it sizzles when you add a drop of water. Use a ¼-cup dry measure to scoop a mound of the mixture into the skillet and flatten the mound into a ½-inch-thick disk with a fork. Repeat with more sweet potato mixture to create enough latkes to fill the pan without touching. Fry each latke until golden and crispy, 2 to 4 minutes on each side. Transfer the cooked latkes to the baking sheets. Replenish the oil in the pan and repeat

with the remaining sweet potato mixture, lining up the latkes on the baking sheets as you go.

5. Transfer the baking sheet to the oven and bake for 20 minutes. Carefully break into a latke and taste to see if the sweet potato is cooked all the way through. If not, return the latkes to the oven for an additional 5 minutes.

6. While the latkes bake, finish the applesauce. Pass the roasted apples and any liquid in the pan through a food mill, catching the sauce in a bowl below. Alternatively, you can puree the apples in a blender or food processor—just peel and core them before you roast them. Serve the latkes hot with the applesauce and sour cream.

PISSALADIÈRE

YEARS AGO, WHEN I MANNED THE COUNTER at a little French café and grocer, I got to make pissaladière all the time. I loved it when the job was assigned to me, as I'd get to hover over the stove top behind the counter, smelling the onions as they caramelized. This classic French tart is so simple and delicious. The onions completely carry it, and the bits of anchovy and oil-cured olives act as little salty oases in a sea of sweetness.

I always make pizza crust at home, but this is one of those rare instances when I think a store-bought pizza crust works well, especially with all the high-quality crusts available these days. Look for something thin and crunchy. With a store-bought crust and caramelized onions defrosted from the freezer, this is an ideal recipe for drop-in guests. It's also quick enough for a weeknight dinner. Oil-cured olives are the black and wrinkly ones at the olive bar. They're my first choice, but a regular kalamata will work, too. The anchovies are pretty key here, but if you'd like to leave them out, double the number of olives. It's essential that every piece has a bit of salt to it.

MAKES ONE 10- OR 12-INCH TART

One 10- or 12-inch pizza crust, homemade (page 220) or store-bought
1 tablespoon olive oil
2 cups Caramelized Onions (page 65)
8 oil-packed anchovies
8 oil-cured olives
2 teaspoons fresh thyme leaves
Freshly ground black pepper

1. Preheat the oven to 425°F.

2. Set the pizza crust on a baking sheet or stone. Paint the top surface of the crust with olive oil. Spoon the onions over the crust, spreading them in a thick, even layer. Leave about an inch of crust empty around the perimeter. Arrange the anchovies in a starburst so that each piece will get one anchovy. Then intersperse the olives between the anchovies. Sprinkle with 1 teaspoon of the thyme.

3. Bake until the crust is golden, 10 to 12 minutes. Scatter the tart with the remaining thyme and lots of fresh pepper. Cut into 8 slices and serve.

CARAMELIZED ONION DIP

ONION DIP HAS BECOME A PARTY TABLE cliché. It's standard on any dried-out supermarket crudités platter, a requisite for Super Bowl, and usually not much of a cause for conversation. It's such a long-lived tradition because the idea is good—a little sour cream, something that was once an onion, a few dried herbs. It has potential, even if it never lives up to it. Well, here's the new version—sweet caramelized onions, fresh thyme, tangy sour cream lightened up with yogurt. It's what I always want onion dip to be. If you have Caramelized Onions (page 65) ready to go in the fridge or defrosted from the freezer, this dip comes together in just a moment. Serve with cut celery and carrots, Kohlrabi Fries (page 58), or just a bag of really good potato chips. I prefer full-fat dairy in general, but this recipe works well with low- or no-fat dairy as well.

MAKES ABOUT 2 CUPS

1 cup Caramelized Onions (page 65)
½ cup sour cream
½ cup plain yogurt
1 teaspoon salt
1 teaspoon fresh thyme leaves or
¼ teaspoon dried

Combine the onions, sour cream, yogurt, salt, and thyme in the bowl of a food processor. Process until the onions are broken down and the dip is well combined. Refrigerate for at least 20 minutes before serving. This dip will keep in the refrigerator for up to 5 days.

JANUARY CRUDITÉS

I FIRST LEARNED ABOUT *BAGNA CAUDA* FROM my friend Lauren, who put Suzanne Goin's *Sunday Suppers at Lucques* into my hands. "The recipes are fancy," she said to me. "But skip to the Bagna Cauda. It means 'warm bath.'" I made it for dinner that night, and I drenched a wide bowl of pasta and broccoli with the salty butter sauce. I had yet to discover my love of anchovies at that point, having only had the gray fillets on bad pizza. But this sauce was salty and silky and richly scented.

A warm bath is exactly the right image for this dish. Vegetables are gently roasted and laid on a row of pillowy endive. And the dip! I chose these vegetables specifically for their ability to hold the sauce. Set the platter in the center of the table and put your heads together as you pick your favorite bites. It's crudités for January, fresh and rich and salty. I like this as a dip, but you can also pour the sauce over the vegetables and serve it as a salad. Feel free to shift up the vegetables with what looks good to you at the store. Just keep a good balance of roasted and fresh.

SERVES 4 TO 6

VEGETABLES

1 small head cauliflower (about 1½ pounds), cut into large florets

4 to 5 thin carrots, halved lengthwise

Olive oil

Kosher salt

2 heads of Belgian endive, Treviso radicchio, or a mix, leaves separated

1 bunch radishes, greens removed, quartered

½ lemon

SAUCE

⅓ cup olive oil

4 tablespoons (½ stick) unsalted butter

2 tablespoons finely chopped anchovies (5 to 7 anchovies, rinsed)

¼ teaspoon crushed red pepper flakes

2 small garlic cloves, minced

1 teaspoon fresh thyme leaves, minced

¼ teaspoon kosher salt

(recipe continues)

1. Preheat the oven to 425°F.

2. Lay the cauliflower and carrots out on a rimmed baking sheet, and drizzle generously with olive oil. Shuffle the vegetables in the oil so the tray gets greased in the process. Sprinkle with salt. Roast until the vegetables are tender and brown in spots, about 25 minutes.

3. While the vegetables roast, make the sauce: Heat the olive oil and butter in a medium saucepan set over low heat. Add the anchovies and red pepper flakes, and stir until the anchovies melt into the sauce, 3 to 4 minutes. Add the garlic and thyme, and remove the pan from the heat. Add the salt.

4. Arrange the endive leaves around the edge of a large wide bowl or platter. Then add an interior row of carrots and cauliflower. Tuck the radishes into the mix as well, and squeeze the lemon over the whole platter. Finally, pour the sauce into a bowl, and set it in the center of the vegetables. Dip directly into the bowl, or serve with a large spoon so each diner can scoop a puddle of sauce onto his or her plate to dip.

CUCUMBER YOGURT POPS

ALTHOUGH WE USUALLY MAKE CUCUMbers salty, they lend themselves to sweetness so well. Sugar actually enhances the cucumberness, and the taste of the vegetable is unmistakable. Pureed, cucumbers freeze and maintain a silky texture, so they're perfect for sorbet, ice cream, and—most of all—ice pops. And because these are packed with cucumbers (vegetables!), yogurt (protein!), and just a little bit of sugar, I have no shame in serving them for dinner on a hot August night. They're barely sweetened, which makes them more of a snack than a dessert, but if you have a big sweet tooth, increase the sugar by 2 to 3 tablespoons.

I have several pop molds, and they're all different sizes. This makes about ten classic-sized pops, but it will make many more if your molds are smaller. You can also rig up your own mold with small paper cups and wooden craft sticks.

MAKES 10 LARGE POPS

¼ cup sugar
¼ cup water
10 to 12 fresh mint leaves
1½ pounds cucumbers (about 3 large cucumbers), peeled, seeded, and cut into chunks
3 tablespoons fresh lemon juice (1 lemon)
¼ teaspoon kosher salt
1 cup thick whole-milk or Greek yogurt

1. Combine the sugar and water in a small saucepan set over medium heat. Bring the mixture to a boil, and let it boil for about 1 minute. Remove the pan from the heat, add the mint leaves, and cover the pan. Let sit for 20 minutes. Strain and let cool to room temperature.

2. Combine the cucumbers, lemon juice, salt, and yogurt in a blender or food processor. Blend until smooth, then add the cooled mint syrup and blend again. Pour the mixture into molds, add sticks, and freeze for at least 4 hours.

ZUCCHINI CHOCOLATE BREAD

ONE ZUCCHINI PLANT. THIS IS MY ADVICE. You only need one zucchini plant. I need *no* zucchini plants because people who didn't take my advice end up dropping off huge club-shaped zucchinis outside my door under the cover of night. I'm not complaining. One big honking zucchini gets me two loaves of perfect zucchini bread. I often grate excess zucchini, pack it raw in freezer bags, and freeze it. Then I get to make zucchini bread in December, too.

This is my standard zucchini bread recipe, and I never get tired of it. It's not too sweet, and the olive oil makes it really light. It has quite a bit more zucchini than the average loaf, so you can really taste it, and the skin creates gorgeous green flecks in every slice. It's such a lovely moist bread, and the flavor really develops as it cools. I love to use whole-grain flour here, but if you only have all-purpose, you can use that alone. This bread also freezes beautifully.

MAKES TWO 8½ × 4½-INCH LOAVES

Unsalted butter, for greasing the pans

½ cup olive oil

½ cup (packed) light brown sugar

3 large eggs

1 tablespoon vanilla extract

4 cups grated zucchini (from about 1 pound zucchini)

2 cups all-purpose flour

2 cups spelt or whole-wheat pastry flour

1 teaspoon baking powder

½ teaspoon baking soda

1 teaspoon kosher salt

2 teaspoons ground cinnamon

¼ teaspoon grated fresh nutmeg

8 ounces semisweet or bittersweet dark chocolate, roughly chopped

1 cup plain whole-milk yogurt

½ cup whole milk

Turbinado sugar, for sprinkling

1. Preheat the oven to 350°F with a rack in the center of the oven. Grease two standard 8½ × 4½-inch loaf pans with butter.

2. Whisk together the olive oil and brown sugar in a large bowl. Whisk in the eggs and vanilla. Add the grated zucchini and stir well.

3. Whisk together the flours, baking powder, baking soda, salt, cinnamon, and nutmeg in a medium bowl. Add the flour mixture to the zucchini mixture and combine with a few swift strokes. It's fine if there are still pockets of flour in the bowl. Add the chocolate, yogurt, and milk, and combine with a few more strokes, taking care not to overmix. Divide the batter between the prepared pans and sprinkle generously with the turbinado sugar.

4. Bake until the tops of each loaf begin to brown and a toothpick inserted into the center of each loaf comes out relatively batter-free, 45 to 55 minutes. (You might see some chocolate, but that's okay.) Let cool for 1 hour before serving.

BUTTERNUT SQUASH CUSTARD WITH BOURBON PECANS

THIS BEGAN AS A GLUTEN-FREE THANKS-giving dessert option, and it proved such a hit with everyone that I brought it into the general fall dessert rotation. It's like pumpkin and pecan pie in one, with the ease and lightness of a not-too-sweet custard. And of course, this is also delicious with pumpkin puree (see page 69). If maple syrup is too pricey or hard to come by, you can absolutely substitute some or all of it with sugar.

If you're starting with a puree that seems watery, strain it through a cheesecloth before measuring.

SERVES 6 TO 8

CUSTARD

Unsalted butter, for greasing the dish

3 cups Butternut Squash Puree (page 69)

4 large eggs

1 cup sour cream or crème fraîche

½ cup plus 2 tablespoons maple syrup

2 teaspoons ground ginger

2 teaspoons ground cinnamon

1 teaspoon freshly grated nutmeg

½ teaspoon kosher salt

BOURBON PECANS

1 cup whole pecans

3 tablespoons maple syrup

1 tablespoon bourbon

¼ teaspoon large flake sea salt, such as Maldon

WHIPPED CREAM

1 cup heavy cream

1 tablespoon maple syrup

1 teaspoon vanilla extract

1. Preheat the oven to 325°F. Grease a 9- or 10-inch square or equivalent baking dish with butter. (A cake pan or pie dish works well.) Have ready a large baking dish that can hold the smaller dish. Fill a kettle with water and bring it to a boil.

2. Make the custard: Beat together the squash puree and eggs in a large bowl. Whisk in the sour cream, maple syrup, ginger, cinnamon, nutmeg, and salt. Pour the mixture into the prepared smaller baking dish. Place that dish into the larger dish, and transfer the larger dish to the oven. Then, with the oven door open, pour the boiling water into the large baking dish so it comes at least halfway up the sides of the smaller dish. (The water won't touch the pudding in the smaller dish—it just serves to help cook the pudding more gently. You're creating a water bath.)

3. Bake until the pudding just barely jiggles in the center, 40 to 50 minutes. Carefully remove the large pan from the oven and take the smaller dish out of the water. Let cool for at least 1 hour before serving. You can also make this up to 2 days ahead and refrigerate. Just wrap it tightly, and remove it from the fridge an hour ahead of time to take the chill off.

4. While the pudding cools, **make the bourbon pecans:** Heat a small skillet over medium heat. Toast the pecans in the skillet, stirring frequently, just until the nuts begin to color, 2 to 3 minutes. Add the maple syrup and bourbon, let them bubble around the nuts, and continue to cook as the syrup first loosens, then gets sticky and gathers around the nuts, tossing to coat the nuts in the syrup, 2 to 3 minutes. Scrape the nuts and syrup out of the pan and into a bowl, and sprinkle with the salt. They will harden as they cool.

5. Make the whipped cream: Combine the heavy cream, maple syrup, and vanilla in the bowl of a stand mixer. Beat with the whisk attachment until the cream holds soft peaks, 2 to 4 minutes. Alternatively, you can beat with a hand mixer or a whisk.

6. To assemble the custard, use a silicone spatula to scrape the whipped cream onto the pudding, mounding it up in a puff in the center of the dish with at least an inch of naked pudding around the perimeter. Top with the bourbon pecans.

CARROT CELEBRATION CAKE

THERE IS AN INDIAN DESSERT CALLED *gajar halvah* that's typically a toothachingly sweet, bright orange pudding of cardamom-infused carrots. I've always loved the idea of it, but I've never been able to re-create it with sugar levels that I could actually consume and enjoy. This gorgeous special-occasion cake—a recipe gifted to me for this book by my friend Carla Blades—takes all the best parts of that dessert and transforms them into a carrot cake that may look like your average carrot cake, but is anything but. The combination of pureed cooked carrots and grated raw carrots creates an incredibly tender and moist cake. It's not too sweet, and the cardamom and ginger perfume the whole thing. The fat here is ghee, which is similar to clarified butter, and it leads to a light and clean taste that is a total surprise if you're used to traditional heavy carrot cake. You can easily make ghee at home (see page 190), or you can buy it prepared at a grocery store. Or, if you would like to use a substitute, try it with melted butter or coconut oil.

**MAKES ONE 9-INCH
DOUBLE-LAYER CAKE**

CAKE
1½ pounds carrots (about 6 large), peeled
Unsalted butter, for greasing the pans
1 cup golden raisins or currants
2½ cups all-purpose flour
1 teaspoon baking powder
1 teaspoon baking soda
1 teaspoon kosher salt
1 teaspoon ground cinnamon
1¼ teaspoons ground cardamom
1 cup (packed) light brown sugar
4 large eggs
2 teaspoons vanilla extract
1 teaspoon grated fresh ginger
1 cup ghee, melted
1½ cups unsweetened grated coconut
Optional: ⅔ cup roughly chopped walnuts

FROSTING
1 pound cream cheese, at room temperature
¾ cup (1½ sticks) unsalted butter, at room temperature
¼ teaspoon kosher salt
1 tablespoon vanilla extract
½ teaspoon fresh lemon juice
2 teaspoons grated fresh ginger
½ to 1 cup confectioners' sugar
Optional: Edible marigolds, pansies, nasturtiums, or violets, for garnish

(recipe continues)

1. Make the cake: Grate ½ pound of the carrots through the grating disk of a food processor or the large holes of a box grater; you should end up with 2 packed cups of grated carrots. Slice the remaining carrots into ½-inch rounds and transfer them to a saucepan. Cover the sliced carrots with water, bring to a boil, and cook until the carrots are tender, 6 to 7 minutes. Remove the pan from the heat and use a slotted spoon to transfer the carrots to a food processor fitted with the chopping blade or to a blender, leaving the hot carrot-cooking water in the pan. Blend the cooked carrots into a rough puree. If they don't break down, add a few spoonfuls of carrot water and blend again.

2. Preheat the oven to 350°F. Grease two 9-inch cake pans, line the bottoms with parchment, and grease the parchment.

3. Add the golden raisins to the hot carrot water. Let soak for at least 10 minutes, then drain through a strainer.

4. Meanwhile, whisk together the flour, baking powder, baking soda, salt, cinnamon, and cardamom in a medium bowl.

5. Whisk together the brown sugar and eggs in a separate large bowl. Whisk in the vanilla, ginger, ghee, and pureed carrots. Add the flour mixture to the sugar-egg mixture and stir with a few swift strokes to combine. Fold in the

coconut, grated carrots, golden raisins, and walnuts, if using. Divide the batter between the prepared pans.

6. Bake in the middle of the oven until the cakes puff and pull away from the sides of the pans, and a cake tester comes out clean when inserted in the center, 20 to 25 minutes. Let the cakes cool for about 20 minutes in the pan before turning them out on a wire rack to cool completely.

7. While the cakes cool, **make the frosting:** Combine the cream cheese and butter in the bowl of a stand mixer and beat with the paddle attachment until fluffy, about 1 minute. Beat in the salt, vanilla, lemon, and ginger. Add the confectioners' sugar in ¼-cup increments, scraping down the bowl and tasting after each addition to bring the frosting to your desired sweetness. Continue to beat until the frosting fluffs up a bit more, 1 more minute.

8. Place one cooled cake layer upside down on a plate or cake stand. Use a silicone or offset spatula to spread a generous layer of frosting over the top of the cake layer, spreading it all the way to the edges. Put the second layer right-side up (so the two flat sides meet in the middle). Pile the remaining frosting on top of the cake, smoothing it out over the top and leaving the sides naked. Leave unadorned, or decorate with the edible flowers, if desired.

SUGGESTED RECIPES
BY VEGETABLE

ARUGULA
[ALSO KNOWN AS ROCKET]
Grilled Beets with Arugula and Chèvre   127

Radicchio and Chickpeas with Creamy Lemon
Dressing   135

Melon with Arugula and Prosciutto   160

ASPARAGUS
Roasted Asparagus with Yummy Sauce   29

Asparagus and Bacon Pasta   182

Gado Gado   224

AVOCADO
Roasted Tomatillo and Black Bean Chili   97

Posole   104

Cucumber Shiso Soba   138

BEETS AND BEET GREENS
Roasted Beets, Julia-Style   36

Miso Greens   40

Winter Borscht   103

Beet and Cucumber Quinoa   124

Grilled Beets with Arugula and Chèvre   127

Polenta with All the Greens   166

Beet and Beet Green Risotto   184

BOK CHOY
Steamed Baby Bok Choy with Sesame   35

Chicken Soup with Lots of Greens   90

BROCCOLI
Roasted Broccoli with Lemon and Parmesan   50

Cheesy Broccoli   51

Creamy Broccoli Salad   134

BROCCOLI RAAB [RAPINI]
Polenta with All the Greens   166

Salty, Spicy Broccoli Raab Pasta   187

Broccoli Raab and Sweet Potato Hash   194

Broccoli Raab and Cheddar Toasts   238

BRUSSELS SPROUTS
Panfried Brussels   77

Shredded Brussels with Crispy Shallots
and Pecans   172

CABBAGE
The Simplest Slaw   59

Hot Sesame Celery with Ruby Cabbage   61

Butter-Braised Cabbage   62

Caramelized Cabbage Soup   100

Posole   104

Napa Coleslaw with Pecans and Peas   132

Braised Kabocha Squash with Miso and Purple
Cabbage   197

Indian Spiced Shepherd's Pie   208

Gado Gado   224

CARROTS
Maple-Glazed Carrots and Parsnips   71

Ginger-Pickled Carrots   74

Roasted Tomato and Vegetable Soup   81

Chicken Soup with Lots of Greens   90

Winter Borscht   103

Butternut Red Lentil Dal   111

Carrot Ginger Soup with Curry Leaves   114

Roasted Vegetable and Cashew Curry   200

Indian Spiced Shepherd's Pie   208

January Crudités   247

Carrot Celebration Cake   257

CAULIFLOWER
Perfect Roasted Cauliflower   63

Cauliflower Cheddar Soup   112

Roasted Vegetable and Cashew Curry   200

Cauliflower Cheese   203

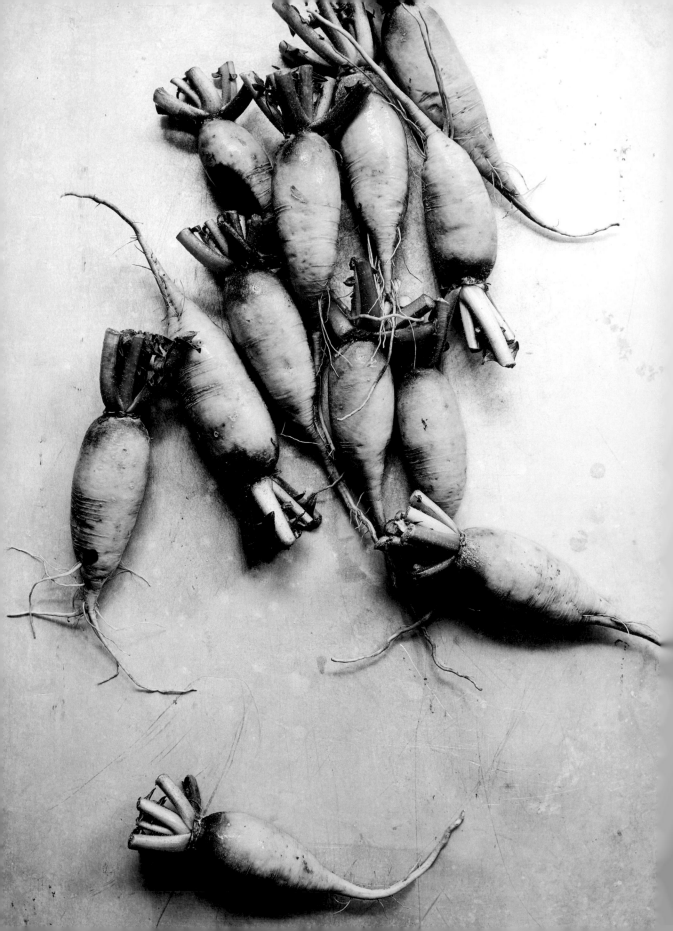

ACKNOWLEDGMENTS

THANK YOU.

To Rob Weisbach, always.

To everyone at Clarkson Potter: my editors Jennifer Sit, Rica Allannic, Ashley Meyer, Angelin Borsics, and Doris Cooper. To Stephanie Huntwork, who has saved the day (and the page) more times than I can even count. To Aaron Wehner, Ada Yonenaka, Kim Tyner, Kathy Brock, Regina Castillo, Meghan Wilson, and Thérèse Shere.

To the amazing team behind the photographs in this book: to Johnny Autry, for always catching the light, Charlotte Autry, for making the food look so good, and to Wyatt Autry, for patiently lending out his parents. To Kali Clark for her skills, to Evan Chender for saving the day with his turnips, and to Susan Hutson for finding gas during the shortage so I could get home from North Carolina. To Paul Fekete for the use of his house, to Curtis at Harris Teeter for his green chiles, and to Herb and Katie Yancey for their tomatoes and their table.

To Max, Maria, and Jess at MX Morningstar Farm for loading up my car with their most beautiful carrots.

To my interns: Soraya Weill for her tasting skills, and to Emma Passy—I can't wait to see what you write.

To the friends who contributed recipes and inspiration to this book: Carla Blades, Mary Natalizia, Jane Kasten, Hedley Stone, Marisa McClellan, Jen Salinetti, Michaele Simmering and Johannes Pauwen, Flavio Lichtenthal, Franck Tessier, Heather Braaten, Molly de St. André, Jean-François Bizalion, and Chase and Alejandro de Onis.

To the friends who offered support through the making of this book: Courtney Maum, Lisa Landry, Alice Goldfarb, Aimée Wimbush-Bourque, Tara Austen Weaver, Bridgette Stone, Lizzie Whitman and Alexander Davis, Dawn Masiero, Casey Scieszka, Margaret Roach, Kate Burke, John McCarthy and Juan Manzo, Emily Kasten and Ben Corbett, and the whole Great Barrington Farmers' Market family.

To Elizabeth Keen, for growing turnips so beautiful that I had to become a food writer to talk about them. To Naomi Blumenthal, for making me write the first word. And to the readers of Eatingfromthegroundup.com, for always asking the best questions.

For recipe inspiration and instruction: Kristin Miglore, Julia Moskin, Alice Waters, Heidi Swanson, Mollie Katzen, Deborah Madison, Nigel Slater, and Suzanne Goin.

I had the great fortune of working with an amazing group of volunteer testers throughout the course of this book. They each contributed so much, and I am grateful for their time, trust, and honesty. Thank you to Anna Hewitt, Natasha Perlis, Mikaela Oldenkamp, Cindy Grob, Christina Auer Shaw, Lisa Cohen, Liz Kellermeyer, Jenn Platzer, Dr. Miranda Haley, Jora Stixrud LaFontaine, Hannah Heller, Jesamine Gilmour, Tori Buerschaper, Beck Drew, Cindy Rosenbaum, Sadie Payne, Marguerite Stoede, Kelly Bancroft, Diana Winarski, Chelsea Marshall, Adrianne Shelton, Amita Baman Tracy, Kendra Vendetti, Holland Gidney, Lana and Michal Osusky, Michelle Boehm, Sarah Rose Moroney, Peggy Greubel, Christina Biedermann, Anastasia MacDonald, Nada Milutinovic, Lucinda Caruso, Kelly Coughlan Gearity, Rachel Oberg, Genevieve Boehme, Marisa McKee, and Mechele Small Haggard.

To my parents, Jamie and Chris Vlcek, for their patience and love.

Over the years, I have gone from being an

only child to having many sisters, both biological and beyond, older and younger, and this crew of women is very present on these pages—especially Lissa McGovern, lead recipe tester and so much more; Janet Reich Elsbach, who has taught me how to ask for help; and, of course, my little (not so little) sister Maia, who is always game for a bowl of buttered cabbage. Thank you.

And to Joey, Sadie, and Rosie, who set the table, do the dishes, and inspire me to end every day looking forward to the next one.

INDEX

zucchini slab frittata, 119–20
Risotto, beet and beet green, 184–85
Root vegetables, 16. See also specific types
   using the greens, 185
Rosemary oil, kale and white bean soup
   with, 108–10
Rutabagas
   Indian spiced shepherd's pie, 208–9

Sage brown butter, 43
Salad(s)
   beet and cucumber quinoa, 124–25
   caprese, 150
   caramelized fennel with citrus and
    ricotta, 170–71
   celeriac, creamy, with maple pecans and
    lime, 202
   chickpea, in endive boats, 219
   creamy broccoli salad, 134
   fresh corn and stone fruit, 145
   frisée with bacon and an egg, 128–29
   gado gado, 224–26
   grilled beets with arugula and chèvre, 127
   kale salad, 56
   melon with arugula and prosciutto, 160
   Napa coleslaw with pecans and peas, 132
   radicchio and chickpeas with creamy
    lemon dressing, 135–36
   roasted tomato panzanella, 155
   the simplest slaw, 59
Salmon
   Swiss chard stem, fennel, and salmon
    fried rice, 131
Salsa verde, boiled new potatoes with, 45
Salt, 18
Sauce(s). See also Butter(s)
   bagna cauda, 247–49
   blue cheese dressing, cauliflower hot
    wings with, 236–37
   creamy lemon dressing, radicchio and
    chickpeas with, 135–36
   feta mint sauce, roasted radishes with,
    180
   for grilled corn, 43
   peanut (gado gado), 224–26
   salsa verde, boiled new potatoes with, 45
   scallion watercress sauce, whole steamed
    sweet potatoes with, 188–90
   tempura dipping sauce, 227
   yummy sauce, roasted asparagus with, 29
Sausage
   big skillet cauliflower pasta, 206–7
   broccoli raab and sweet potato hash
    with, 194–95
   and Swiss chard strata, 175–76
Scallions
   scallion crepes, 216–17
   scallion watercress sauce, whole steamed
    sweet potatoes with, 188–90
   Swiss chard rolls, 213–14
Sesame oil, 19
   hot sesame celery with ruby cabbage, 61
   steamed baby bok choy with, 35
Shallots
   beet and beet green risotto with, 184–85
   crispy, shredded Brussels sprouts with
    pecans and, 172–74

shallot butter, 32
Shepherd's pie, Indian spiced, 208–9
Shiitake barley soup, 92–93
Shiso
   cucumber shiso soba, 138–39
Slaw
   Napa coleslaw with pecans and peas, 132
   the simplest, 59
Soba, cucumber shiso, 138–39
Soup(s), 80–115
   butternut red lentil dal, 111
   caramelized cabbage, 100–101
   carrot ginger, with curry leaves, 114–15
   cauliflower Cheddar, 112–13
   celeriac and apple, 106–7
   chicken, with lots of greens, 90–91
   corn chowder, 96
   Hakurei turnip, 87
   kale and white bean, with rosemary oil,
    108–10
   nettle, 84–85
   pea, 88
   posole, 104
   roasted tomatillo and black bean chili,
    97–98
   roasted tomato and vegetable, 81–83
   shiitake barley, 92–93
   winter borscht, 103
Spinach. See also Greens
   big skillet cauliflower pasta, 206–7
   creamy, with dill, 30
   roasted vegetable and cashew curry,
    200–201
   shiitake barley soup, 92–93
   spinach soup, 84–85
Squash. See Summer squash; Winter squash
Strata, sausage and Swiss chard, 175–76
Summer squash, 16
   grilled, with basil ricotta, 142
   melted zucchini toasts, 239–40
   zucchini and garlic scape pasta, 122–23
   zucchini chocolate bread, 252–53
   zucchini slab frittata, 119–20
Sweet potato(es), 16
   and broccoli raab hash, 194–95
   latkes, with roasted applesauce, 242–43
   simple sweet potatoes, 66
   whole steamed, with scallion watercress
    sauce, 188–90
Sweets
   butternut squash custard with bourbon
    pecans, 254–55
   carrot celebration cake, 257–58
   cucumber yogurt pops, 251
   zucchini chocolate bread, 252–53
Swiss chard. See also Greens
   chicken soup with lots of greens, 90–91
   miso greens, 40
   polenta with all the greens, 166–67
   sausage and Swiss chard strata, 175–76
   Swiss chard rolls, 213–14
   Swiss chard stem, fennel, and salmon
    fried rice, 131

Tacos, poblano rajas, 157–59
Tatsoi
   chicken soup with lots of greens, 90–91

Tempura nests, green bean, 227–28, 229
Toasts
   broccoli raab and Cheddar, 238–39
   escarole and preserved lemon ricotta,
    241
   melted zucchini, 239–40
Tofu
   gado gado, 224–26
Tomatillos, 16
   roasted tomatillo and black bean chili,
    97–98
Tomato(es), 16, 148–49
   caprese salad, 150
   freezing roasted tomatoes, 155
   millet-stuffed, 147–48
   radicchio pizza, 220–21
   roasted, butternut squash lasagna with,
    191–93
   roasted tomato and vegetable soup,
    81–83
   roasted tomato panzanella, 155
   tomato Cheddar pie, 151–52
Tools and equipment, 20–22
Turkey, ground
   roasted tomatillo and black bean chili,
    97–98
Turnips and turnip greens, 16, 185. See
   also Greens
   caramelized Hakurei turnips, 27
   Hakurei turnip soup, 87
   scarlet turnip galettes, 230–31

Vegetables. See also specific types
   buying, 11–13
   cleaning and storing, 15–17
   complementary ingredients, 18–19
   freezing, 15, 16, 17, 44
Vinegars, 19

Watercress
   chicken soup with lots of greens, 90–91
   nettle soup with, 84–85
   scallion watercress sauce, whole steamed
    sweet potatoes with, 188–90
Watermelon radishes with herb butter,
   235
Winter borscht, 103
Winter squash, 17, 67
   braised kabocha squash with miso and
    purple cabbage, 197–98
   butternut red lentil dal, 111
   butternut squash custard with bourbon
    pecans, 254–55
   butternut squash lasagna, 191–93
   butternut squash or pumpkin puree, 69
   maple-baked, 67
   seeds, roasted, 70
   smoky Delicata chips, 73

Yogurt
   cucumber yogurt pops, 251
Yummy sauce, roasted asparagus with, 29

Zucchini, 16. See also Summer squash
   and garlic scape pasta, 122–23
   melted zucchini toasts, 239–40
   zucchini chocolate bread, 252–53
   zucchini slab frittata, 119–20

Library of Congress Cataloging-in-Publication Data
is available.

ISBN 978-0-451-49499-3

eBook ISBN 978-0-451-49500-6

Printed in China

Book and cover design by Stephanie Huntwork

Cover photography by Johnny Autry

Food styling by Charlotte Autry

10 9 8 7 6 5 4 3 2 1

First Edition

33614080543183